TALES FROM THE OLD COUNTRY ESTATES

Also available in this series:

Tales from the Old Country Estates

John Bailey

LARGE PRINT

Oxford and Orlando

First published in Great Britain 1999
by David and Charles Publishers

Published in Large Print 2000 by ISIS Publishing Ltd,
7 Centremead, Osney Mead, Oxford OX2 0ES, and
ISIS Publishing, PO Box 195758,
Winter Springs, Florida 32719-5758, USA
by arrangement with David and Charles Publishers

British Library Cataloguing in Publication Data
Bailey, John, 1951–
   Tales from the old country estates. – Large print ed.
   1. Manors – Great Britain 2. Country life – Great Britain
   3. Large type books
   I. Title
   941'.009734

ISBN 0-7531-5797-7 (hb)
ISBN 0-7531-5798-5 (pb)

Printed and bound by Antony Rowe, Chippenham and Reading

CONTENTS

The Country House in our Time

The decline of the English country house was rapid: after a golden age the position of the country estates plummeted as the 1870s progressed. The situation deteriorated during the 1880s as Britain faced increasing competition from the world food markets. Refrigeration and steam-engined boats meant that all manner of agricultural produce could be brought from the Commonwealth especially to the British market, and as a result agricultural prices in the UK toppled. Income from the land, so vital in maintaining country estates, began to prove insufficient, and the whole fabric of the English countryside began to change as a result.

This is not an exaggeration. For generations the English country estate had wielded immense power, political and social as well as economic. For long periods Members of Parliament had depended on the patronage of the landowners, and the judiciary and even the Church were also to a greater or lesser extent under their sway. In those changing times, however, the new rich — almost invariably industrialists — might well want to buy a country house, but not the vast estates that went with them: for them a thousand acres, or at the most two thousand, would almost certainly be sufficient. Land did not really interest them other than as something to shoot over, so new wealth was never going to save the traditional landed country estate.

A common solution was for the landowner to sell the farms to the tenants, and this was often what happened. For example, at Gunton in Norfolk the twenty thousand acres had almost entirely gone by 1914 — ultimately leaving the house itself even more impoverished than it had been before, of course, since the purchase money was soon spent and the rents stopped coming in.

At times these problems were made worse by conspicuous over-indulgence. To quote the case of Gunton again, far too much money was spent on shooting and entertaining — even if the guests *were* royalty! Some houses economised, of course, but others did not, and it seems that these were content to go down in a blaze of glory. World War I also made its mark, since very few able-bodied men returned in 1918 from its terrible carnage. Moreover, as the twentieth century has progressed, the more egalitarian political system has made it increasingly difficult for the old estates to survive as they once did. Yet another blow to those still clinging to survival was the agricultural depression of the 1930s; and for many, World War II was the death knell. A number of large houses were taken over by the army or by evacuated schools, and some never recovered after 1945.

Naturally this tale of woe has had a sad effect on the staffs of country houses over the past century or so.

What I have tried to do in this book is to choose those estates that have adapted, and do survive. This seems to have been the secret, for those estates and landowners who have refused to comply with the changes forced upon them have, in most cases, gone under. I chose to go to houses that have weathered the storm, because of wise, far-seeing management. Some houses, such as Gunton in Norfolk, have been developed as private dwelling places, subdivided into flats and houses; others have become institutions, perhaps housing offices or even hospitals; and others such as Caer Beris in Wales have become hotels. Those that are still owned by their original families have, in virtually all cases, learned to open their doors to the public — often, as in the case of Chatsworth or Beaulieu or Knebworth, with very dramatic and exciting results.

It is exactly the same with the staff, and almost everyone I have interviewed has, like the houses themselves, adapted and survived. A century or more ago the hierarchy in country houses was very rigid: the "servant" did his or her job and no other, and job descriptions were immutably fixed. This sort of hierarchical set-up is no longer possible, however, and to work in a country house today demands flexibility. Moreover in almost every case, the people involved do not find this a hardship: after all, flexibility means breaks and changes in routine; it demands thought and initiative — and it is, in truth, exciting.

So, for example, we will look at Patti Razey at Knebworth, a lovely lady who has had six or seven jobs at this beautiful house and is still trying out new ones!

We will meet John Savill at Syon House who has never quite known what his job was, and to this day continues to turn his hand to others! And we'll talk with men such as Frank Widdop at Harewood House who is officially a butler but still drives the Earl of Harewood to every home game that Leeds United play at Elland Road! So times have changed, but those staff who have been able to change with them have generally flourished. The nice thing is that every single member of staff interviewed in this book has wholeheartedly spoken up for his or her style of life, clearly demonstrating that great wells of happiness still exist in the country estates of today.

What of the future? Will it still be possible to write a book at the end of the twenty-first century on those working in country estates at that time? Well, there is no doubt that the whole question of the future of country estates is a complex one — but equally, there is no doubt that the owners of grand houses do feel more confident in the future. As we enter a new century they know that life is not going to be easy, but there is a commitment to continue — and that, obviously, is good for all who work with them.

Life in country houses today is easier both for the owners and for the staff. Telephones and faxes have vastly improved communications, and in virtually all cases, owners have adapted; for instance they no longer live in the great state rooms but will have a sensible dining-room next to a modern kitchen . . . good news for butlers and cooks alike! So, whilst a house may still appear grand to the general public going round, there will be areas within the structure well adapted to family use.

Finance is still a nightmare, however. Grades I and II listed buildings of huge size are not repaired cheaply, and costs are soaring all the time. There are grants available from English Heritage, but these are not massive, and lottery funding is not necessarily a solution either, because quite rightly, no lottery grants are given to private owners unless major public access is guaranteed. Moreover it is important to realise that public visitors do not really make money for estates in most cases. Owners might say that they would not be there but for the public, but what they generally mean is that the public pays for the upkeep and repairs, but little more besides — and what generally happens is that owners have to look for more diverse ways of keeping the estates, the houses and their staff afloat. Many have their houses licensed for civil weddings, and corporate events can bring in good money. Film and TV companies often pour money into the coffers, especially when there is such a desire for period drama — and there is a fair bet that the house will be redecorated, too!

This is all good in many ways: the house is saved and the jobs of the staff are safeguarded; and just as important, the house reverts to its original role as a place central to the local and wider community both. Country houses are now playing an important role in the life of the countryside again — and the general feeling is that the private owner is their best custodian. This is largely because he or she will have a deep and special love and understanding that has been passed down and nurtured through generations. And staff love working for the old families — people who have a real sense of the past. When houses are put on the market the contents are often sold, and this upsets the whole balance and feel of these extraordinary places. Furthermore, if a rock star pays two million pounds for a house, and perhaps spends a further million renovating it, it is very unlikely that he or she will allow the public access. Certainly both the National Trust and the Historic Houses Association believe that houses are best kept in private hands if public access is to be guaranteed. And by opening to the public, the role of these houses into the next century is guaranteed, and no one can accuse them of being dinosaurs.

All this is great news to those staff members who are willing to adapt, willing to be like Patti Razey and take any occupation that comes along, increasing job satisfaction as a result. Also, ties between master and servant have become looser and freer, more in accordance with modern times. In short, there will be room in country houses for those who want to work there in the future. There will be exciting occupations available — occupations that the servants of a hundred years ago would never have envisaged. In fact it is quite possible — and I say this with guarded optimism — that the future of country houses and those who work within them is exceptionally bright. Let us hope that history proves me to be correct.

It has been a joy to write this book: living on a country estate myself, I feel that I have some bond at least with all these people who have been good enough to give up their time and share their memories. Country estates are, and always have been, special places both physically and spiritually removed from the general run of human life; yet all life is here, and I hope you enjoy meeting all its characters . . .

Gunton Park

I first stumbled around the decaying building of Gunton Park in north Norfolk nigh on forty years ago. As a child I adored fishing the lake just to the south of the hall, and typical of any small boy, would set off to explore once boredom had set in. At the time I didn't know that the estate had been owned by the Harbord family since 1676, that the house had been largely rebuilt in the mid-eighteenth century, and that Brettingham, Adam and Wyatt had been involved architecturally just as Repton, Bridgeman and Gilpin had contributed to the design of the park itself. No, all I saw were acres of water, fields and woodland all mysteriously quiet and deserted, a playground paradise for a six-year-old.

Many of the buildings in the main complex were without roofs, trees were growing through the walls, windows were broken or missing, and doors swung eerily open. The estate churchyard was overgrown, but although buildings in the walled garden were in decay, I once saw a gardener there who looked up and shouted — and I ran away. How would I know that in years to come I would actually live in that very place?

In 1980 the hall, the surrounding buildings and much of the park were sold by the Harbord family. An amazing auction of the hall's contents took place, realising hundreds of thousands of pounds and attracting dealers from all over the world. The young architect Kit Martin bought the fabric of the place: he had a vision of Gunton reborn, of a place once again bustling with life. Had he not stepped in when he did, the hall and the stables, the game larder, the audit house — just about everything — would have fallen into complete collapse. However, a massive restoration programme was undertaken, to exemplary conservation principles, so that little by little the buildings were restored until someone from the year 1800, let us say, would hardly have noticed any significant change.

The buildings were sold off, and my wife and I were amongst the steady stream of buyers; we bought a corner of the walled garden, a long thin building that once comprised the apple store, the gardener's cottage and the garden's potting sheds. Looking south and surrounded by high walls, the garden feels warm year in, year out, even in winter when storms are beating against the Norfolk coast, only half-a-dozen miles to the north.

So what is life like in a country estate today, at the dawn of the twenty-first century? Let us first consider the physical aspect, and in particular the antiquity of the buildings. Tangible history stands all around — stones you can touch, courtyards that echo to the sound of your feet. Here there is beauty and serenity, but individuality too — take the quaintly shaped buildings in the brewery yard, for example, the octagonal game larder, the classic row of cottages a few metres to the north, and to the west, the graciously curving single-storey building that looks out across the lakes. The Adam chapel is magnificent, as is the façade of the hall itself with its great windows, columns and flag above, fluttering in the wind. Behind this lie the remains of the library, gutted by fire in the 1880s; but to the west is an inhabited wing, featuring the former ballroom, an impressive cube of a room which probably gives more space than any other private sitting area in the country. Above, to the north of the park, rises the observation tower, built at the turn of the nineteenth century as a lookout point for any massing of agricultural labourers threatening revolution: from it you can see Norwich to the south and coastline all around.

The church, too, has been beautifully renovated, and services are held at Christmas, Easter and harvest time: these are often special times with most of the residents assembling to sing and pray together, and then afterwards racing across the lawns for a seriously fantastic afternoon tea!

However, the beauty of Gunton lies as much in its atmosphere. What impresses visitors first and foremost is the quietness: this is a landscape in a time warp, still set before the combustion engine, and even today there are probably more horses than cars on the estate. Space, too, is very precious in today's crowded England, yet here the park covers 1,800 acres, with tracks and paths everywhere, leading from one wood to the next over streams, beside lakes and even into the Deer Park. And for wildlife, Gunton is truly an oasis. Wild deer proliferate, there are foxes, badger setts, stoats, weasels, passing otters and bird-life in profusion. There are ponds of newts and toads, and even populations of ancient, near-extinct wild carp.

Forty years ago when I was a child, Gunton was a haven for my rambles, and so it is today. Perhaps because so much of the park is private, the children living here can walk, play and cycle on their own in perfect safety. It would be wrong to portray Gunton as a paradise on earth, of course. Disputes there are, naturally enough, but most remain within containable limits and are settled for the good of all; and the parties, although not particularly frequent, are memorable — summer parties especially, when the sound of music and laughter drifts through the trees. At such times it is not difficult to feel a sense of history rippling through the warm night air.

Ruby Fisher, Farmer's Wife

I have never claimed to know Gunton properly: even after forty years I still have only a scattered specific memory of what has gone on. To get any real idea of its past, you must talk to a resident of longer term.

The walk to Ruby Fisher's cottage is delightful. Leaving my own house at the walled garden and turning right, you go through that narrow strip of woodland call the Slip. When I went it was a wonderful early summer morning, with dew on the grass and the sky a startling blue above the waving canopy of trees. If you are observant you can pick up signs of where the night visitors have been: for instance, deer have obviously passed along one of the avenues because their hoofmarks are quite fresh and the dew is still scattered. There's a strong smell of dog fox urine at a junction of the paths, a sweet, musky smell which will hang for days. On the field to the north, rabbits have woven trails almost everywhere, just as though the field has been laced with spidery webs.

After perhaps half a mile, the Slip gives way to that vast expanse of land known as the East Park. On its limit stands the Tower, and a little lower down, the Elderton Lodge. But I have come to visit the cluster of houses around the Dairy Farm, and most specifically Ruby Fisher's delightful cottage, surrounded by flowers that are all aglow in the early morning sunshine. A hundred yards opposite Ruby's present gate stands the Dairy Farm itself, large and imposing, well set off by a maze of outbuildings. This is where Ruby lived between 1945 and 1982: the smaller cottage to the side of the farm is where she moved in 1940, and lived for the first five years of her married life.

The Fisher family has had connections with Gunton for nearly one hundred years. Ruby's father-in-law moved to Dairy Farm at the turn of the present century; John Fisher, Ruby's husband-to-be, was born there and went to school at nearby Paston Grammar in North Walsham. Ruby lived at Cromer at this time, the well-known seaside resort four or five miles to the north on the Norfolk coast. Her mother ran a guest house there, and in those days Cromer was considered an upper class, even an aristocratic resort. Though Ruby would never describe her family as wealthy, they were well-to-do, and Cromer was a town humming with life, especially in the summer.

She and John met after he returned from Canada. The farm at Gunton was well manned and his father had had no real need for him, so John had set off with Fred Gibbons, another park resident, to seek fame and fortune in the New World. John only returned after several years, just before his father fell ill and died in 1930. By the time Ruby married John in 1940, he was in charge of the farm and the war had already started. It was a change of life that she did not immediately relish:

"When I first came to Gunton I thought I'd died, honestly! You've got to realise that Cromer was quite a bustling town, and the guest house was always full of life. And I belonged to every single thing that was going. I'd learnt the violin from the age of nine, and at around fifteen or sixteen I began to sing. I'd cracked the little finger of my left hand which made playing the violin difficult, and after all, singing is easier — for example, you don't have to worry about strings snapping when you come into a warm hall on a cold night!

"Anyway, I joined the Choral Society, and then began to tour with the Norwich Philharmonic. I can remember the audition clearly: it was held at Chamberlain Hall on St Giles, and I was given a page of Verdi's *Requiem* to sing in Latin. I don't know how I did it, but I got through, and I was in! I remember my number in the orchestra was a hundred and twenty-one!

"At the start of the war I was still singing everywhere. I was brought up a Methodist, but that didn't stop me singing in every denomination of church you can think of. By now troops were billeted all over Cromer and on Friday nights I used to sing for them. Sometimes we'd have a pianist, but sometimes there'd be a member of the Guinness family there — I can't remember his name, though I do remember he was a round, cuddly fellow! — and he used to play the 'cello very nicely; I think we worked rather well together. And if I weren't singing, then I'd be helping down at the YMCA serving out food for them — always chips and beans as I remember!

"So, after dashing here and there all my life, I came here to this sleepy little place tucked in deep into the bog. And it was the war, so I couldn't even ride my bicycle at night without the lamp being all masked up and dimmed. We moved first of all into the tiny cottage behind the farmhouse. The idea was to stay there just for a few weeks until my mother-in-law moved out . . . in the end we stayed there for five years! It was a tiny little place, nowhere as luxurious as it is now, and I had to bring up two small children there. There was no electricity, no bathroom, *nothing* — so you can see why I felt my life had almost come to an end.

"Later on in the war I was heard by one of the Robinson brothers — very big in radio then — at one of my rare singing engagements, and they tried to get me to become professional. The idea was to go for an audition in Bedford — I think I was going to be on a radio programme called *Ring Up The Curtain!* Anyway, I went back to the farm to talk the idea through with John, and his comment was that there were three good reasons why I shouldn't even think of going, namely him and the two boys! Well, it was about the only time in our life that we had anything remotely like a cross word, and we weren't much more than civil to each other for a while after that, I can tell you. I suppose today there would have been no doubt whatsoever in my mind: I would have been a star! It was around that time that Vera Lynn rose to prominence — and I never really liked her very much, if the truth be known. The boys always used to say to me it was because she'd got my job!

"The war changed the park a very great deal. Remember, it had been laid down to just grass and trees for centuries, and now there was the clamour for food, so great swathes of it went under the plough. The cricket pitch was one of the first areas to go, and that was particularly sad; we begged those on the war committee to let the pitch remain. After all, we argued, it would be lovely for our brave boys when they came back home to have a cricket match to look forward to. But no, it had to go, along with all the rest. It was John himself who actually ploughed the first furrow across it: 'I've had many a good game on that pitch,' I can remember him telling me, 'so let me be the first to put a furrow across it.'

"In fact we didn't have a lot of time for many of the committees in those days. When the East Park was ploughed up they insisted that the standard amount of fertiliser should be spread on the ground. Of course, we argued that the land had been enriched by the sheep for centuries and was quite fertile enough. But, once again, no, we had to do it their way. Well, the inevitable happened: the corn just grew and grew, and then it flopped. It was a wet summer, too, and so it just lay in great heaps all over the place. It was the job of the POWs in the area to keep turning the stalks day after day to try and get them to ripen on the ground. But the rain kept coming, and if there *was* any sun it was all watery and couldn't repair the damage. The whole lot mildewed and rotted. What a waste that was. All the way right up to the Tower was just this rotting corn — I can see it and smell it to this day.

"My mother-in-law wasn't too fond of the war, either. She was a very particular sort of lady who liked things just so. She'd been used to quite a lot of help in the Dairy Farm, and she'd been brought up grandly as a young girl. Now, with the war, we all had to open up our doors to evacuees. Don't get me wrong, we did this quite willingly, but it did cause a problem, too! Ours came from a very rough area of London somewhere around the docklands, I can't remember the exact place now; and these poor people came up from London to Yarmouth by boat, would you believe! Then they came overland to Cromer, but when they arrived the children were all still seasick. There were two women who were pregnant and one of them had a miscarriage the very first night. If that wasn't bad enough, she quite ruined her feather bed . . .

"But it was in the morning that the worse problem started. To get to the toilet, just an earth closet in those days, you had to go out of the back door, past various outbuildings for a way and finally be able to relieve yourself! When my mother-in-law — 'Granny' as they liked to call her — told them all about this, they just looked at her in amazement. 'Don't worry about that, we'll go anywhere!' they told her. And they did!

"Well, what were we to do? They really would go everywhere, even in the places where we were making butter and cheese and stored the milk. John had to go up to the hall to see Lady Suffield about it. When Elsie, the cook, laid into him for not bringing any milk, he just replied that he'd explained everything to her ladyship: 'You wanted to see me, Fisher?' 'I'm afraid we can't supply you with any milk or dairy produce any more. I'm afraid it's just not hygienic.'

"Well, no sooner said than done, and those evacuees were moved into a cottage of their own further off into the park.

"I think it's quite possible there are unexploded bombs here in Gunton. It's a famous episode, very well recorded, about how a German bomber jettisoned its bombs one night very close to the house here; you can still see the craters they made to this day. The exploded bombs were taken away the next day by the army and prisoners of war, just the two of them. Now, although Granny Fisher was deaf, she absolutely swore that she felt *four* bombs drop, not just two. She always maintained it, and was totally convinced about it; but where they are now, goodness only knows.

"Whilst the war was on, the men from the Worstead Signals used to come into the park and set up just outside the Dairy Farm. They would often appear just before going off abroad, and they'd put up their few kitchens and tents on a Friday night, generally after dark. But it was in that area that we always used to store the manure, great heaps of it; when they arrived they obviously thought they'd found a nice warm area to stay in, and it wouldn't be till daylight they'd see the reason for it.

"We got to know the officers very well, and John would always collect some eggs for them for breakfast. They appreciated that, and we found it paid dividends. In the first place, whatever food they had left over at the end of the weekend they'd pass on to us. We used to get liver, beautifully prepared, and then huge, 7 lb cans of baked beans; I'd parcel them all up into smaller quantities and give them out to friends or round the park in Cromer. The other bonus was that we never got our eggs or anything else pinched! I remember very well that Arthur Jones, who lived next door and who was a gardener, had no end of his eggs pinched. The Clarkes — he was the blacksmith — who lived opposite also used to lose eggs, and in the late summer when the plums were ripe, all his best fruit.

"The park was still a busy place in those days. Apart from Jones there were also Sambles, Doughty, Hardingham and Williamson in the gardening team. Mind you, this was nothing like the fourteen gardeners there'd been earlier on in the century, but it was still quite a lot of manpower. I've already said that Mr Clarke was a blacksmith, but he also used to mend clocks and watches, and the men used to come on a Sunday morning to his house for a haircut. The carpenter, Mr Barber, lived on the right-hand side of the Tower; on the left was his sister. Billy Ward was a foreman on the estate, and the painter was Ralph Ward; Ralph was disabled, and it turned out that this was through lead poisoning because there was so much lead in paint in those days. Fred Gibbons — you remember that he'd been to Canada with John — came back, too, and he was the beater and bricklayer around the place. Of course, everybody used to help out and do things on the estate that needed doing.

"None of us really did badly during the war, I suppose, because we were surrounded by animals and poultry — we even used to make about 20 lb of butter a week, both for our own use and to give away to family and friends. The dairy was always going, and John continued with his milk round. We had about sixteen Friesian milking cows, and ran about forty steers. John always said the pasture wouldn't take more, and anyway, it was quite enough for us."

One of the joys of talking to Ruby — apart from her brightness, hospitality and strength of welcome — is the vividness of her memories. Buildings that you think you know were obviously quite different, even half a century or so ago; take my own house, for instance:

"Of course, where you live now, John, is quite different from how it used to be. Then, everybody used to go through that door next to your present front door into what was called the bothy. You'd go through that room with just a beaten earth floor and would be out into the walled garden. It was a magnificent place in those days, with spectacular apples, peach trees, nectarines, cherries . . . you name it, it'd be there. That's where I first met Miss Doris Harbord, the sister of the last Lord Suffield to live in the hall itself. It's only those who didn't *know* Miss Doris would say harsh things about her. Of course, you had to remember who she was — after all, she'd once been a bridesmaid with the present Queen Mother — but provided you talked straight to her, she'd always respond.

"I remember once asking her about some crab apples, great juicy things just outside where you live now; I had the mind to jelly them you see. 'That's quite all right, Ruby,' she said. In the end we collected the crab apples together and split them fifty-fifty.

"The first time I ever saw Miss Doris was in the bothy itself. She had just been in to feed the chickens [I can attest to the fact that they're still to be heard every summer morning at 5am!] and was still carrying the maize, and behind her was a whole posse of child evacuees, following her like the Pied Piper.

"There's lots and lots I could tell you about the park — just so much that's almost all been forgotten. You know that big fir tree standing outside the church door, to the right with the plaque? Well, the plaque isn't actually original! The real one was stolen in 1980 when there was the big auction at the house, and this is just a fake. Kit Martin had to ask around till he found somebody who could remember what the exact inscription was. As you know, that tree was planted by the Princess of Wales in the 1870s. But what you probably didn't know was that there was a similar tree to the left. That was planted by none other than Kaiser Wilhelm, the Emperor of Germany during World War I! Anyway, on the outbreak of hostilities, the men from the estate got their saws and got rid of the tree; support for the boys overseas, they called it!

"Those were the great days of Gunton, when the park was a byword, I suppose, for revelries and royal goings-on. There are even some trees down one of the approach roads today that were planted by Franz Joseph, the Emperor of Austria himself.

"Of course, everybody round here knows about the visits of the Prince of Wales before he became Edward VII. Rumour runs riot! Lily Langtry came here to visit him, and he used to put up one of his mistresses in a posh Cromer hotel! And it was all down to the Prince of Wales that there was the huge fire here on the night of 18 December 1882 — I know that date because it was my father's birthday! I don't know if I should really tell this, but it's what Granny Fisher always used to swear happened. It's a bit of a mystery, the fire, and always has been, but she was convinced that it came about in the following way:

"It was a great honour, of course, to have the Prince of Wales at Gunton, and Lord Suffield — the one that was Miss Doris's grandfather — was his *aide-de-camp*. The only trouble was that he was not a cheap man to entertain. He'd want to shoot thousands of birds each day, and of course he'd bring a vast retinue of friends and courtiers with him; the wine cellars emptied at a rate of knots. Everything about his visits was expensive. Mr Allen, who was head gardener in those days, said that the Prince and Lord Suffield would gamble on anything, absolutely anything; he once told Granny Fisher that he watched them bet on two falling leaves, on which would reach the ground first!

"Anyway, back to 1882: Lord Suffield himself was in India when the agent got a letter from the Prince of Wales' household saying that he wanted to come to Gunton for the Christmas shoot. Now, this was a problem, really because the estate was beginning to run short of money, due to the prince himself more than anything. Still, it was also difficult to refuse the request, even though the estate couldn't really afford it. A lot of extra staff would have been needed, but it was very hard to think of an excuse. Now, Granny Fisher swears that the following idea was cooked up to get them out of it. She didn't know where the idea came from, whether from the agent, or from Lord Suffield himself, or whoever, but it was carried out and it went sadly wrong.

"A maid was instructed to burn just a bit of paper in the corner of a bedroom. The idea was that there'd be some smoke damage and Lord Suffield could reply to the prince that it was impossible for him to come because of redecoration. Everybody thought there'd be no risk attached to this, and even if the fire did get out of hand, well, there was a fire engine on the estate itself. However, they'd never tested it, and it seems that the lake, with all that water, was just too far away and the hoses wouldn't quite reach. It was a disaster. The fire raged and got out of control, and a man was sent on horseback to Cromer for the big fire engine there. Granny always says he didn't come back until the next day! By then, of course, it was way too late and half the hall was burnt down, and most of it hasn't been put back to this day. I can't tell you whether that's true or just gossip, but at least the prince and his party didn't turn up that Christmas."

It was time for me to leave, and Ruby waved me off. I walked back through the park, now happily being put back to its original grassland due to the efforts of Kit Martin, Ivor Bracker up at the observatory tower, and Charles Harbord, son of the present Lord Suffield. What a delightful lady — but then, she always had been so. A little way from the area where Ruby has lived for nearly sixty years stands a small lake called, appropriately enough, Fisher's Pond. What few residents know is that this lake is actually quite famous in the fishing world, because it has a stock of original native English carp. This was known about by eminent fishermen back in the 1950s, and one of them, the celebrated author known as BB, wrote about his visit to the lake in a letter to his fellow anglers:

"Permission to fish the Pond was given readily enough by the charming farmer, Mr Fisher. I had a great day at the Pond for it is set in the most beautiful countryside. I also caught many a fish — most not large, but all of the long, old English variety. Later in the afternoon, Mr Fisher's wife, a lovely lady, called me over to the farmhouse and in the big, cool kitchen there she treated me to a splendid afternoon tea. It was the kindest of gestures and made the whole affair seem quite perfect."

Beaulieu

Of all the great houses, perhaps none has made such an attempt to capture the visitor as Beaulieu: although the undoubted beauty of the house, the abbey and the grounds still exists Lord Montagu has obviously set out to open his grand house to the public on a very large scale. Most notably, Beaulieu is now the home of the National Motor Museum.

As Lord Montagu writes: "Showing my home and welcoming visitors to Beaulieu since 1952 has been a source of great pleasure to me and their visits have ensured that Palace House, Beaulieu Abbey and other historic buildings in my care are in a better state of repair now than they have been for many decades. I hope that they will survive for many years to come, for future generations of visitors from all over the world to enjoy."

Certainly, a tour of Palace House, historic seat of Lord Montagu's family is a delight indeed. It could well be corny — but it isn't: two lovely ladies dressed in period costume explained how the house was run back in the nineteenth century, during the Victorian period. The lady dressed as the housekeeper of that period, Mrs Chadwick, was particularly interesting. A crowd of visitors, many American, flocked around her as she guided us around the house.

It was Mrs Chadwick who had supervised all the female servants and had run the house on behalf of the present Lord Montagu's grandparents. It was her task to keep the accounts and ensure that the larders and cleaning cupboards were kept stocked, that the house was clean and the linen cupboard full. The title "Mrs" was a courtesy for, like most housekeepers, Jane Chadwick was unmarried.

Directly under Mrs Chadwick in house hierarchy was Mrs Hale, the cook. She produced meals in accordance with Lord Montagu's grandmother's wishes, working under conditions that cooks today would find trying to impossible!

Next came the footmen and maids — Palace House had three footmen whose job included cleaning the knives and lamps which they also lit, cleaning shoes and boots and carrying coal and wood. One of their most unusual tasks was to scrub clean the small silver coins carried by the ladies of the period.

The maids were divided by areas in which they worked. The most senior was the lady's maid who, like her male equivalent, the valet, was responsible for taking care of Lord Montagu's grandmother's clothes, hair and jewellery and helping her dress in the elaborate costumes of the period. The two housemaids spent most of their time above stairs, cleaning the house, making the beds and lighting the fires, but the kitchen maid and scullery maid were confined below stairs. The former did much of the routine preparation and cooking of food for the cook, whilst the scullery maid simply washed up. Laundry maids were traditionally identified by their red hands and the laundries were found well away from the main living quarters because of the steam and smell.

Generally speaking, servants' hours were from 6am until 10.30pm or whenever the owners of the house retired. Each week they were given one evening and half a day on Sunday free, together with one free day a month.

Any of these might be stopped if work was not up to standard. They were also issued with one candle a week and a uniform, which if it wore out before the appointed time, was replaced by stoppages from wages. These varied considerably, from the £25 to £30 a year a butler might hope to earn, to the £5 to £9 earned by the scullery maid.

As our "modern" Mrs Chadwick made quite clear to us all that day, every servant knew the limits of his or her position and whilst conditions of service may seem unreasonable to us today, for many, in those days, the security provided by such steady employment, in such an attractive home, was immeasurably important.

Fred Sheppard, Butler

Lord Montagu quite rightly believes that Beaulieu is setting an exemplary standard when it comes to recording the history of great houses, and in the John Montagu building is housed the most impressive of archives. Susan Tomkins was the archivist at the time of my visit, and she greeted me with the hospitality for which Beaulieu is rightly recognised. She led me through endless corridors filled with tomes from the past, and certainly had a treat in store for me: many years ago, the elderly butler, a certain Fred Sheppard who had served during the 1930s, had been interviewed on two separate occasions, firstly when he was well into his eighties, and again when he was in his nineties. His most fascinating of stories begins and ends in Hampshire, but it has many interesting adventures along the way; I can do little better than to relate it as he has recorded it, in his own words:

"I was born in Salisbury in 1904, and had six brothers and sisters. My father worked on the Longford estate as a carpenter, often making fences, and we lived in an estate cottage. He was there altogether for thirty years. In those days you simply took what job you could find, and there was virtually no choice really open to anybody like us.

"The house was crowded, and before the Great War, I went off to live with my grandmother. When the war broke out, boys aged thirteen or over could be engaged fulltime on the land and could leave school. I was fed up with education anyway and joined the local gardeners, and never went back; I guess they were glad to see the back of me! I certainly never regretted having a more formal education. Then, in 1917, I became a messenger around the Salisbury area and that's how, in 1919, I came across a job: a local butler at Stockbridge needed a boy to help him and I became his assistant. This is how I came to work for Sir Frederick Bathurst: I enjoyed the job, and henceforth never really left service. I was trained very well and it was fine for me. I got away from home and became myself, knowing at last what I wanted to do.

"That's how my life jogged on until the early 1930s when I came to Beaulieu. The vicar's wife told me that the Montagus were looking for a butler so I decided to apply for the job. I was called for interview by Lady Montagu at her aunt's house in Wilton Place, London. Well, I caught the train and I decided to walk there. Soon, though, being a stranger to London, I realised I was going to be late so I decided to take a taxi. I got in and put my bowler hat on the seat beside me. Well, we hadn't been going more than a mile or so when, believe it or not, we had a scrape with a van. The taxi driver and the van driver got into a violent argument — there was no separating them so I slipped out of the taxi, fearing I would be late, and ran all the way to Wilton Place. Just as I got there, all hot and sweaty and completely flustered, I realised that I'd gone and left my bowler hat back in the taxi. Now you must realise that to arrive for an interview for a butler's position in such a state of undress would at the least cramp my chances. However, I got the job, and so went on down to Beaulieu — and felt I'd never seen any building quite so lovely. You remember that phrase, 'that peace which passes all understanding'? Well, for the first time in my life, I could appreciate it. I worked at Palace House, and in all my time there I was totally happy.

"I enjoyed life at Beaulieu right until the war broke out, when I was roped into the ship-yard at Hythe. We got plenty of food in the factory and I quite enjoyed life there, air raids and all. I went back to Beaulieu after the war, but on a temporary basis; work wasn't really fulltime there any more, and so I had to help out at local hotels. It was then that I decided to go into window cleaning and had the idea of a vacuum chimney sweep! I did that for a while even though I was still living in Palace Yard back here in Beaulieu up in the woods.

"Looking back to the 1930s, Beaulieu was a friendly place to work. We had several cooks between 1933 and 1939, but in particular I remember Mrs Percy Adams — she would cook up some wondrous stuff. Alice and Eleanor were the head housemaids, and the cook would always have two assistants. My assistant was a lad called Joe Spedding, and he really was on the lowest rung of the ladder here at Beaulieu. Times were a bit tight in those days so there was no housekeeper as such: the cook did all the ordering, and if I needed any stores she would get them for me as well. As I remember, there were two shops here locally and we'd buy from them on alternate weeks so we showed no favouritism; of course, they've long since gone, replaced by supermarkets. I remember one of them was run by a Mr Whimsey who was also head of the fire brigade here at the hall.

"Also in my time was Harold Bryant, the carpenter on the estate who would repair cottages and do any jobs in the house when needed. He was based in the estate yard, which is now the Fairweather garden centre.

"During those years, to say my time off was a bit scanty would be the understatement of all time. My wife used to say, 'If your children met you in the street, they wouldn't know you!' If the truth be known I was never home till way past dark, way past the time my two boys were in bed. Occasionally we'd go to flower shows, and sometimes we'd go to look at the ships in Buckler's

Hard; we'd walk or bike, but that was about the limit of our time off.

"Even when I wasn't working I had to join the fire brigade and help with all the training. You see, it was the butler's job to be on hand if any fires broke out in the house itself. I was particularly worried about the staff because their rooms were right at the top of the house and I couldn't really see a way down safely for them if a fire should break out. Then we decided they could come down the secret stone staircase to the drawing room and go out of the door or windows there. We were fairly sure that would be safe because it was all made of stone.

"Ironically I was responsible for the only fire that ever broke out in my time there! It was Christmas and I was burning holly in one of the downstairs grates. I put on too much and the chimney set on fire. It just wouldn't go out, and the walls in the bedrooms above got absolutely baking hot. We 'phoned the fire brigade who came and put the fire hose down the chimney and created the most dreadful mess you've ever seen. And all this at Christmas time, too!

"One of the biggest jobs I had was helping with the preparations for any special occasions. You'd have to clean the silver till it gleamed. We had a few pieces stored in the bank, but all the usable silver had to be cleaned and polished constantly, and especially before any important guest came. Then the glassware, too, till it absolutely shone.

"There was no rest even when the Montagus were away, because then I was called on to do other jobs. In particular it was down to me to clean the windows, which was quite a job, as you can imagine; I had to clean them outside and inside, even though you might expect that to be the job of the housemaids.

"In all my time at Beaulieu I was always called Sheppard, never Fred. In actual fact my mother had called me Hector, a name which I've dropped all my adult life, preferring Fred which was made up for me. You see, back in my first job, in my footman days, I was called Frederick because that was how it was in every country house: the first footman was always called Frederick! And the second footman was always called Charles, whatever his name was. So that's how I came to be called Fred, and I've never dropped it since.

"I kept record books as a butler or, rather, an extended diary of day-to-day events: all the people who came as guests, all the amusing events, all the problems with the staff — everything was noted down. In fact, many butlers did this. Unfortunately, I don't quite know where mine have got to now.

"The staff dining room here at Beaulieu was very typical of those I've worked in in all manner of houses. However, it wasn't really very strict, and the meals were pretty informal — if you ask me, the code here wasn't strict enough. At Beaulieu we didn't stand on any sort of ceremony, and males and females all ate together, though the kitchen staff would eat in the kitchen so they could carry on with their work. Weekends were especially busy because you'd have more visitors who would come down from London to enjoy the countryside air. Christmases were absolutely hectic because the house would be full of extra guests — Lady Montagu had four nephews who always came to stay, and her step-sister also had children, so there was quite a crowd. They all brought their chauffeurs and their attendants — but I never had more staff to help me, even though I'd have liked a good few!

"In those days I always wore a black coat with a waistcoat and striped trousers in the morning. In the evening it was a ritual that I'd put on a tailcoat, and on very special occasions I'd sometimes wear a white waistcoat with a white bow tie. These uniforms were not provided, you know, and I'd buy them at second-hand shops around the area; there were some that specialised in butlers' clothing. The cost would depend on the quality of the cloth and the overall condition. A suit of clothes could be as much as £5 which was quite a lot when you consider that when I started at Beaulieu I was only earning £90 a year. Mind you, that was considered very good at the time, though my wages stayed the same all the way through the thirties whilst I was there.

"Life at Beaulieu in my time was fairly modest, and a typical dinner party would not have a menu of any great note. We'd generally start off with soup and follow that with fish or meat. Then there'd be dessert and then fruit. The wines were particularly my job. Lady Montagu kept the cellar key and gave it to me simply when it was needed. There would certainly not be wine with every meal, and they'd often go for weeks without having any. I remember it came from London dealers, and some was laid down for years. Sherry was frequent at dinner parties, and sometimes there'd be port.

"We'd have nothing remarkable in terms of glasses, but oh, my word, getting the silver right was really something. Joe Spedding would clean it with his hands, a wash leather and then polish and polish and polish. The big thing was trying to get the scratches out. That was the art — it wasn't a question of polish, it was a case of getting the cutlery smooth. You know, I spent all my life watching the clock, and that's often been because of some damn scratch or another. As a young footman myself I could spend all day cleaning a single spoon. I suppose it's almost impossible for people to imagine in this day and age, but that's how it was then.

"A typical working day would see me on duty at around seven o'clock in the morning, and perhaps knock off around ten in the evening or sometimes later. Of course, things varied, but these were the general times, especially when the family were in residence; I might have two hours off in the afternoon, but this didn't really let me have much of a social life. I don't think I ever went to the cinema during all those years, not even once, and you've got to remember that cinema going was the big hobby of the day!

"The House children were always having birthday parties, and I can tell you that was a devil of a job! We'd have to move all the big chairs out of the dining room, and put in small ones for them. Afterwards they would go to play in the upstairs dining room and then we'd have all the clearing up to do, once they had all gone, and that could take most of the night!

"Having said all this, I wouldn't want you to think by any means that it was a dull or unsociable place to work in — far from it! I loved my time at Beaulieu because it was a warm house and rich in stories. There was one in particular I liked, that we called the venison story. Lord Montagu used to work in London and would come down for the weekends; on one particular weekend he was given a great haunch of venison which was too fresh to eat. His instructions were that the cook should prepare it for the following weekend. However, then he was ill and didn't come down for a fortnight,

"That night there was no venison, and he asked the cook where it was. She told him that they'd thrown the venison out. 'Thrown it out! Where?' The cook said that she'd asked the gardener to bury it because it had gone off.

"Well, Lord Montagu leapt up and went off to see the gardener to find out where he'd dug it. The haunch of venison had been put in the dung heap — but Lord Montagu asked for a spade and he dug it out and hung it on an apple tree, then hosed it down and finally took it into the kitchens. Well, the cook simply refused to cook it. 'You'll cook that venison or it will be the last thing you do in this house!' said Lord Montagu. As you can guess, it was cooked — and they said it was the best venison they'd ever tasted!

"Lady Montagu's remarriage was also a big and joyful event; we were always afraid that she wouldn't find anyone else. The catering was done by a London firm. The marriage took place in Beaulieu church and the reception was here in the house and I had to organise that. It was my job to announce the three hundred and fifty or so guests and I had them waiting by the front stairs where Lady Montagu would come down to greet them. The problem was that the happy couple decided to come down the back stairs! I'd got everybody prepared at completely the wrong end of the house! However, I managed to swop everybody round and bring them through in the right order, and the day was saved.

"There were embarrassments, too . . . I remember one night I was preparing a dinner party for twelve. There were six people staying in the house and three couples were coming in from outside, two of whom I knew well but the third I'd never met at all. Everybody had arrived — all the ones I knew, that is — and then there was a knock on the front door and a very smart man and woman were standing there. Obviously I invited them in, assuming them to be Mr and Mrs Smith, the people we were waiting for — and the ones I didn't know. I took them through to the drawing room and announced them as such — and there was total confusion! Lady Montagu looked at them and then at me and declared in surprise: 'This isn't Mr and Mrs Smith!' she said. And surprised they replied, 'No, we're Mr and Mrs Jones and we just came here to ask directions!' There were hoots of laughter, but I wished I could have dropped into a hole! If my memory serves me properly, Lady Montagu asked for another two chairs to be put at the table and we had fourteen for dinner that night! That, though, was typical of Lady Montagu, who was one of the kindest, most warm-hearted people I've ever worked for.

"There were other nice things about working here at Beaulieu — for instance I used to fish a lot in the river. I had a small boat which I kept moored up in the trees, though I never used to catch very much; I did far better fishing in the pond behind the house that was stocked with trout. I used to take the present Lord Montagu fishing there, when he was a child, and there would be a real hullabaloo if he got his feet wet.

"There was also seine netting on the river every year, about three or four times each summer. Of course, we didn't have nylon ropes in those days, and those old heavy hemp ones made for hard work, even for six great men. It was up to me to organise the team, and we wouldn't attempt a trip unless we'd got a full complement. The fish were generally mullet or bass, or sometimes sea trout — the mullet were given around the village, the bass and sea trout stayed in the house! We also put some crab pots out, and had those once in a while.

"After the war, as I've said, I worked a little bit more at Beaulieu, cleaning windows and doing all sorts of odds and sods. And then my life changed yet again, and on a really major scale. There was a society lady here that I knew quite well, a woman called Mrs Varley. An old friend of hers was going off to America to run the British Embassy in Washington, and evidently he was having great trouble finding a butler — and Mrs Varley, bless her, decided that she knew exactly the right person for the job: me. So she came back and I was offered the post as butler to the ambassador at the British Embassy in America!

"Links with Beaulieu were maintained whilst I was over in the States. I met Lord Montagu at the Yacht Club at Palm Beach and actually waited on him at a dinner over in the States whilst he was on a visit. I remember it was a sweating hot day, the temperatures well up into the nineties. I had to carve the ham, and I was hot and perspiring like a fountain, but I couldn't, obviously, wipe my face; so I would drop something on the floor on purpose so I could bend to retrieve it, and would then wipe myself with a napkin, hidden under the table!

"America was certainly an interesting experience, and I met a great many important people over there — including Sir Winston Churchill, whom I found to be a terrific man. He liked his wine, his cigars and a really good joke. I remember on one occasion all the members of the embassy staff went for tea on the royal yacht when it was in the harbour. I was told the story that on the Duke of Windsor's accession to the throne he went as king to the boat. He observed that the curtains were shabby in the stateroom, and said he would like them replaced. The head steward had to go to the Ministry of Works with the request, and was asked why the king wanted new curtains; he replied: 'Well, that's easy. They were made in Queen Victoria's time. They were turned in King Edward's time. They were cleaned in King George's time and now the new king has decided he wants some fresh ones!'

"I retired, finally, when I was seventy-one, and I'd had enough of it all by then. Looking back, I can see both ups and downs as a butler in the twentieth century. It was good to be in contact with some cultured and interesting people, and I also enjoyed a really good standard of living all the way through my life, especially in America. I lived in some lovely places, too. Of course, there were downsides; in Britain especially there are some people that treat any servant like a piece of furniture — you might just as well not exist for them, and I've never liked that. You are also on call twenty-four hours a day, and this is no exaggeration! You might think that you'd knocked off late at night, but there was always the possibility of accidents or a fire, and it was your job to see that the right people were called. I don't think there's a butler's wife in existence who would choose a butler for a husband the second time around, and I've never encouraged my children to enter the profession, or even to think about it!

"I suppose my twenty-first birthday is a pretty good example of what I'm talking about. I was a footman at the time and I remember it was a wet Sunday. The family I was working for were golf crazy and they came in from the course wet and dirty. Or course, I'd already made them tea, then I had to make them supper and then I had to clean and dry all their clothes. It was midnight exactly when I got to bed, and I didn't even have time to drink my own health because I knew I'd have to get up at six o'clock the following morning. That was my twenty-first birthday! Nor do I think I ever had a Christmas Day off for over fifty years when I was a butler — but that's just the sort of thing a butler has to put up with. It's a style of life that's like no other; but looking back over the life I've led, I guess I would say that on balance it's all been worth it."

Berkeley Castle

Berkeley Castle stands just above the flood plains of the River Severn and is a truly a magnificent building. Years ago, Miss Gertrude Jekyll described it as follows: "Berkeley is like some great fortress roughly hewn out of natural rock. Nature would seem to have taken back to herself the masses of stone reared centuries ago. The giant walls and mighty buttresses look as if they have been carved by wind and weather out of some solid rock-mass, rather than wrought by human handiwork.

"When the day is coming to its close, and the light becomes a little dim, and thin mist-films rise from the meadows, it might be an enchanted castle, for in some tricks of the evening light it cheats the eye into something ethereal, without substance, built up for the moment into towering masses of pearly vapour."

Some might say that this is over-imaginative, but all those who have seen the castle, and especially in the evening light, comment on its awesomely atmospheric presence. The history of the castle, too, is equally impressive: the history of the Berkeley Manor goes back to the reign of Edward the Confessor in the mid-eleventh century, when it was held by Earl Godwin, father of King Harold. After the conquest Godwin was obviously despoiled of his possessions, and Berkeley was handed over by William the Conqueror to William Fitzosbern, Earl of Hereford, to hold as a western defence of the new kingdom against the Welsh Marcherlands across the Severn.

The strategic value of the site on a dominating hill was recognised, and it was strengthened by building up the existing mound and setting up a stout wooden stockade. This elementary fortress was probably demolished around 1088 during a time of rebellions, but the site was too important to abandon and Fitzosbern's provost, Roger, calling himself Roger de Berkeley, was given the task of supervising a new construction. Three successive Rogers followed, and little by little the castle that we see today began to emerge. The second Roger entertained Henry I during the Easter period in 1121, which presupposes that there must have been at least some kind of lodging for the king and his retinue.

Such are the origins of Berkeley Castle, and the Berkeley family can therefore now boast of having held it in their possession for over eight hundred years, during which time it has become very much a part of the fabric of this country. It has featured in a Shakespeare play; a King of England — Edward II — has been murdered within its walls; a breach was battered in its defences by Oliver Cromwell, which exists to this day: this is Berkeley, rugged, dramatic, and you cannot begin to understand it unless you appreciate its position as a type of architectural bastion of authority raised to mediate over the disputes between England and Wales.

During this eight-hundred-year period Berkeleys have obviously come and gone, living to some extent the lives of country squires, leading a peaceful rural life. But they have also been men of action, not cruel, not brutal, but striving to keep the peace during turbulent periods. Berkeleys throughout the centuries have been nicknamed "Make-peace", "The Wise" and "The Magnanimous", indicating a civilised family holding sway through uncivilised times over the centuries.

Mollie Sage, Long-Time Helper

Mollie Sage started work in the tearoom in Berkeley Castle in 1956, and has served the estate in various capacities for forty-two years. She, too, thinks of the castle as a fairytale place: "Over the years I've grown to love the castle deeply. Above all, I really love the look of the place, especially at sunset when it is quite different to any other building. The pink sandstone was taken from the valley of the River Severn and it really glows. It's also amazing to think that it was made in times when men had hardly any of the equipment and tools that we have today."

I met Mollie Sage one summer's afternoon shortly after she had moved into a charming cottage on the Berkeley estate just outside the village. With justifiable pride she showed me the back garden that she was building, and the delightful rooms that she had recently had decorated, all with windows looking out onto the small green. Mollie's father, Jack Sage, was known as the Grand Old Man of Berkeley:

"My father served in several capacities here at Berkeley — as stable lad, groom, gatekeeper, riding instructor, he turned his hand to just about anything that needed to be done — and he's almost certainly its most famous servant. There was something about Dad, you see, that inspired the imagination. He was such a character, and worked here for so long that everyone knew his name. Mind you, life wasn't easy for him. He was born in 1869 and his parents — my grandparents — died when he was only a young man, leaving him pretty well alone in the world; this meant he never had much schooling. He worked with horses, here on the estate, from the age of twelve — this was where he made his home. His early jobs were pretty rough — he would be expected to muck out the stables, to brush down the horses, to carry in their food and do all the menial tasks that are involved with them. But all the time he was learning, getting to know them, and becoming an expert with them.

"A few years later he ran away from Berkeley to join the 28th Gloucestershire Regiment; he served in India and in Ireland, and then went on to take a really active part in the Boer War. When he was discharged he came back to Berkeley to work as a groom for the Hunt. Of course, life was disrupted once more by the Great War, and in 1914 he was recalled. With hindsight, we know about World War I and its grim trenches, but at the time, you see, the generals still believed it would be won with horsepower, and so Dad's knowledge of horses, and his skill with them, was highly valued by everyone.

"Although he'd had a terrible wartime career he was an understanding man, happy to listen to people, never flustered, and telling his own stories when he judged the time was right. Back home at Berkeley he became a founder member of the British Legion here in the 1920s and served through World War II as an air-raid warden, complaining because he was too old for active service.

"Here at Berkeley, father worked for four owners: for Lord Fitzhardinge until 1916, for the Earl of Berkeley until 1942 and then in his latter years for both Captain Berkeley and finally Major Berkeley. Through most of the early twentieth century he worked at the castle as head groom, and his particular responsibility was to have them fit and ready for the hunting season, and well turned out for each hunting day. Hunting has always been important to the family; long ago the Berkeleys were involved with royalty and politicians, wars and politics, but latterly they became more closely identified as country squires, deeply concerned with their hounds and horses. Traditionally the hunting season would start at Berkeley, then everyone moved lock, stock and barrel to Oxfordshire, and finally they moved on again to Gerrard's Cross to hunt the London countryside. They would then move back in stages to finish up at Berkeley once more. Many horses were needed for such an operation, and Dad was constantly on the go, travelling backwards and forwards, making sure that fresh animals were ready when required, and that those which had been hunted were rested, fed and looked after. He obviously had a large staff, and he used to say that everything was planned like a military operation.

"My dad always taught any children connected with the castle to ride. Like any large estate, Berkeley has always had an agent to oversee the general day-to-day running of the place, and teaching horsemanship to the agent's children was always my father's responsibility. He just adored horses and animals of every sort, but he was also a particularly gifted teacher, and very good at showing children how to treat these big animals with respect and love. Sometimes he would go hunting himself, though on these occasions he would be responsible for the Berkeley children, looking after them and showing them the way. He simply loved all the colour, the noise, the action and the smells of the horses.

"Dad's wages weren't much, and he wasn't given a great deal of time off — not that he wanted it. His life centred around the stables here, living on the estate, being a central part of it. Of course, some of the horses became very dear to him indeed; naturally he had his favourites, which he would groom and exercise himself. But more than that, my dad was famed for mucking in with everyone, always happy to help out and to do any job that helped the stable routine run smoothly. It was a lively place all right, in those days when I was so small. I can still remember the smells, the sights and the constant clattering of hooves, the horses whinnying and their banging against the stable doors. There always seemed to be activity everywhere, lads coming and going, riders leaving or returning and horses everywhere you looked. Magic times. My dad's head was constantly awhirl: there were horses to be shod, groomed, fed and exercised; the tack to be sorted, cleaned and kept in good repair; the stables to be maintained — the dirtied straw had to be removed every day; and the stable lads had to be kept happy and contented but still hard at work. It's a wonder I ever saw anything of him at all!

"Down by the Severn there used to be a place called the Gallows, and there an old man would put down any horse that had come to the end of its useful life. He had an old sledge to move the carcass, and he'd cut the meat up down there and it would all be left lying around on the ground. When he had a mind he'd take it back up to the kennels for the hounds. It was a dreadful place, full of rats and flies.

"It might seem strange to you that a man who so loved horses could ride with the hounds and kill the foxes. But you've got to remember that in those days — as now — people saw hunting as a part of a whole way of life — and foxes did a tremendous amount of damage all over the land that we're talking about. When I was little — I remember it well! — our neighbour had ten hens: one night, he heard a terrible squawking, and saw the fox leaving amidst a whirlwind of blood and feathers. There were only two hens left.

"The problem with shooting is that the fox can lie injured for days and this only brings about more suffering. Nobody could feel more strongly for animals than I do, but I still support hunting. The Hunt still meets on the green, just here outside the window.

"Because Dad was a resourceful man, all sorts of jobs came his way. When I was just a little girl I remember a particular piece of excitement here at the castle. Men would use a net for salmon down on the Severn when the fish were running and one day a colossal sturgeon got caught in one of the baskets; it just couldn't get out, and thrashed around dragging the nets behind it. The men went down and were appalled when they found what they'd caught. Still, they struggled with it onto the bank and killed it — and then found out it had to be sent up to Buckingham Palace because sturgeon are royal fish! This task fell to my father, to take it to Buckingham Palace during the night. He covered it over with a sheet and put it in the back of an old van; but as he was driving along a police car pulled up alongside him; they began to look in, and what they saw just looked like a body. So they pulled him over and questioned him, but when they pulled back the sheet they almost collapsed when they saw what was under it!

"My dad used to help with the corn harvest, too. He was really good at training dogs, and I remember one in particular, a terrier called Nipper. Dad would take Nipper along, and as the last strands of corn were cut, the rats would break and run — but Nipper would be on them all! Not fair to the rats, you'd say? Well, you ought to see the damage they can do during the course of a winter. Rats used to be the bane of a farmer's life, because not only would they get into the stored grain and eat it, they'd foul the rest, too. Rats can also cause untold damage to the structure of the barns themselves, constantly burrowing under the foundations, and gnawing at the beams and the doors.

"In those days — and this was long before there was any expensive machinery around to help us — we'd all turn out at harvest time to lend a hand. Dad would be there with a horse or two, carrying people around or helping to pull out any cart that got stuck in a sodden hollow. These were lively times all right. Even us children would be there, doing what we could — though more often than not getting into some mischief or other!

"In later days, Dad became the gate-keeper here at Berkeley. Of course, his duties weren't as difficult and dangerous as they probably would have been centuries ago when the castle was a place of frequent violence, but it was still a job of some responsibility. Security at Berkeley has always been an issue, and it was Dad's job to watch carefully everybody that came and went. And, of course, he had to look smart and attentive, too! The gatekeeper is the first person that any important visitors see when entering such a grand house, and he always considered it an honour to be chosen for the position.

"The castle has two entrances, one for the public and one for the family, and my father used to pride himself on being the family's gatekeeper: he loved to open up the double doors when he saw them coming, and to let them in — no one else ever dared pass. I remember that he had a dear little lodge with a fireplace, and he was happy to bide there nearly all hours of the day. He had a cupboard and a table and he'd sit in there as happy as anything!

"My father really liked the tourists who flock here during the season. Of course, they're a relatively new development but no one minds either them or the money they bring. All big houses like Berkeley are looking for new forms of income, and it's good to see the amount of enjoyment visitors get. I enjoy the hustle and bustle of the summer as well, and I work now in the public tearooms, which can get pretty hectic at times — everybody needs their cup of tea after a long walk round the castle and gardens.

"My father would walk round the castle, sometimes wearing his medals, always talking to the visitors, telling them the stories of his past and of the castle's. Both are equally dramatic, I think. After all, this place has seen the death of kings, conquests and all manner of bloodshed, and so did my dad. Yet both my father and the Berkeley family have always been essentially people of peace, of wisdom, and it seems to me that it's just been outside influences that have pushed them into ways they haven't always wanted to go.

"My dad died when he was ninety-six, back in 1965. He finished work in the gatehouse on Friday night, and through Saturday and Sunday complained that he didn't feel well — and that was most unusual for my dad. He'd never had the doctor out in his life, but the doctor did come and diagnosed indigestion. Dad went to bed, and he didn't get up again. By the Monday his mind was wandering: he was complaining that he was going to be late for parade, so I just said, 'No Dad, you're not going to be late — you'll be the smartest man on the parade!'

"Well, he opened his eyes and said, 'That's how it should be' and then he died in my arms. I like to think that he was happy to the end.

"My own life at Berkeley has been very varied, and I've done all sorts of things in my forty-two years here. As I've mentioned already, I started in the tearoom in 1956 and helped serve and cook for private dinner parties — I've even waited on Prince Charles himself.

"The job I've liked best has been baby-sitting for the Berkeley children. I attended the wedding of Major John and Mrs Berkeley, and always adored baby-sitting the two boys that soon came along. Of course, there were nannies, but they seemed to come and go and I used to step in to take their place. I used to love taking the children off to the zoo, or even having them round to stay; they used to say that they liked being in an 'ordinary house'. It was a real treat to go up there for an evening when the Berkeleys were going out; I'd always be handed a glass of gin to see me through the night! I've never had children of my own but I love those boys as though they belong to me. I wouldn't want you to think I take anything for granted here and I would never take liberties. I've always got the greatest of respect for the family and they've been very kind to me, for somehow I've grown to think myself as very close indeed to them.

"I suppose some of my earliest memories are of the castle just before World War II. The Earl who died in 1942 became the owner at the end of World War I. He was very eccentric and to begin with, very short of money. To help his financial situation he sold off Berkeley Square in London, and this made him a millionaire. He then married an American lady from Boston, Massachusetts, who was fabulously wealthy in her own right. She had spent a lot of time in Italy and brought back an Italian chauffeur to the castle. They toured around in a distinctive yellow car — I can't remember the make, but it was certainly most exotic for the Gloucestershire countryside! They had a footman and an under-footman, both of whom wore the traditional Berkeley livery of green and yellow. There were four people working in the kitchen, and four even in the pantry; there were also four housemaids and four

49

under-housemaids plus a hall boy and a butler. This was a large staff for this day and age, but then the Countess adored the place and was prepared to spend a lot of her own money on its upkeep. Being an old building, Berkeley constantly needs repairs of one sort or another, and the Countess was keen to see these carried out. A lot of her money went on repairing the roof.

"She was an artist and she had a studio half way up the hill, and also a summerhouse down on the banks of the river, which she used to visit in a pony and trap. Those were great days, and there was always life and colour around the castle, which was really the centre of life here. I was at Berkeley Junior School, and remember well that whenever the Countess was in residence in the castle she would organise a party for the school children. A marquee would be put up, and we would be marched from the school two at a time, crocodile fashion, through the door of the castle and out into the enclosed grounds. It was always a lovely party, and the Countess provided everything you could think of for us.

"There were pageants on the lawns outside the castle and people used to dress up in fantastic costumes. These were great local occasions and we all adored the colour and excitement. Sometimes scenes from the castle's history would be re-enacted, with lots of trumpet-blowing and colourful uniforms. A great many men worked on the Berkeley Estate, too, well over twenty in the sawmills and in the forest, and the place was almost self-supporting in produce, with teams of gardeners; once a week a gift of vegetables would be sent to the hospital in Berkeley.

"Of course, many estates were self-sufficient in those days — they simply had to be because transport was less reliable and more expensive. The sawmills, for example, produced all the timber that was necessary in the castle, for the outlying buildings, estate cottages and for constructing fence posts. A great many posts were needed for paddocking, especially.

"The Countess was a wonderful person. In the war years she opened up the castle swimming pool to the American soldiers — you can guess how the local girls loved that! During the week she would assemble all the ladies from the village and take them up to her studio, and for hours they would sit there knitting squares of wool to make into blankets for soldiers on service.

"There have been various alarums and excursions here over the years. In the old days we were often cut off by the river, and had terrible times with flooding: the meadows would all go under water and we'd have to walk backwards and forwards through the flood to get home; as children, we would wander around in the water looking for fish that had become marooned. Sometimes when I was coming back from secondary school, the public bus would drop us off and then I would have to wait for the Berkeley cart horse called Rabbit to ferry me back home. One day the bus was late and Rabbit had already made his last journey and I had to stay the night on the other side of the river. But we all used to love that sort of thing. Back here around the castle everybody used to swap food for days because they couldn't get out and buy any. We were all like one big happy family.

"Of course, there were characters, too. Back in the time of the Earl and Countess, there was a certain Captain O'Flynn — either the agent or the secretary, I can't remember which — and he liked his drink. One night the Earl and Countess were in London, and the Captain had hit the bottle a bit. Now, there was a great bell in front of the castle kept there for emergencies, and the Captain decided that, for a bit of a joke, he would ring it just to get all the staff onto the lawn. Well, he rang the bell and all the staff roared out in their night-clothes, carrying their most precious belongings, thinking there was a fire — all except for the young Italian boy whom the Countess had adopted and who was living in the castle; he couldn't be found anywhere. O'Flynn was terrified and everybody began to search the castle from top to bottom. They finally found him sitting in the kitchen, because he had thought the bell was ringing for supper!

"The Hunt ball here at the castle has always been a great occasion and I have always been around to do one job or another. One year, well over a quarter of a century ago, I was on the ladies' cloakroom, when there was a bomb warning. The police were there in no time telling us to evacuate the building, and immediately there was a mad panic, the women dashing for their coats and their handbags; the trestle tables with the coats on collapsed, and there was the biggest heap of fur coats you have ever seen! We just had to ask them to be calm and to go out in the grounds where we'd issue them with blankets. It was obviously a hoax but the anti-Hunt feeling has stepped up over the years. About six years ago I was once again to attend a Hunt ball, and was advised to go early because of possible trouble. So that is what I did; but when I got to the churchyard in front of the castle, a crowd of saboteurs rushed from the graveyard waving banners and banging at the doors. I could see that the big double doors of the castle were closed, shutting me out, and I started to panic — but then I remembered how calm my father would always be in the face of any crisis, and it helped me keep calm. Then suddenly the police were there: they let me into the castle and I was safe. It was as though my dad had been looking after me.

"Being connected with a great house and a family whom I have grown to love has given me very great satisfaction indeed. I have often been alone here in the castle at night with perhaps just the boys sleeping up above, and I have detected a real presence, a real atmosphere. I am not saying the place is haunted in any way, but it is somehow as though history is alive, as though the past is still not forgotten. I like to think that I will be a part of that past, and that my own spirit will always be here."

Chatsworth

Like millions of others over the past centuries, I fell in love with Chatsworth in my youth. I remember well the day that I was first taken there, by car from the city of Manchester into a park of unparalleled beauty. So vast, so regal, so perfect in its setting of woods and hillsides, I can remember the emotions to this day. The spell lingers on, and at Christmas time each year I travel north to fish for grayling in the Derwent that winds its way in front of the great house. I say "fish", but more often than not I simply sit, spellbound. Winter is a very special time to see Chatsworth: the park is quiet, and the light is frequently magnificent, especially towards sunset when the last rays glint on the hall as though the very structure were set afire. Sometimes when the day is calm you can stand by the banks of the river and the building is mirrored perfectly in the water. In winter, too, the pollarded willows glow a vivid scarlet, a colour that lights up the dreary Derbyshire sky.

As I have said, I am one of millions for whom over the centuries Chatsworth has provided a cherished haven, a perfect retreat; this has been largely for those who work in the great industrial northern cities that circle the estate. To call it an estate is really inaccurate — rather it should be considered a kingdom, because even today Chatsworth is surrounded by thirty thousand acres, and at the height of its prosperity controlled well over twice that amount. It is this history of hospitality that makes Chatsworth so important and so special to those that love it. In the preface to his guide book the Duke of Devonshire writes: "I would like to say how very welcome all our visitors are to Chatsworth. A house and garden of this size needs people to bring it to life, so my family and I, who are lucky enough to live here, are delighted to share our pleasure with you." His sentiments have been echoed over the centuries — indeed, Chatsworth has been opened to visitors ever since it was first built. Daniel Defoe, for example, wrote about it in the eighteenth century, and in 1775 an inn was built at the nearby village of Edensor for the convenience of the sightseers.

In the eighteenth century the family lived mostly in London, but the housekeeper still had instructions to show people round, and when the fifth duke was present there were "open days" when even dinner was provided. But it was the sixth duke, perhaps more than anyone, who brought Chatsworth into the public ken, and the following extract from *The Mirror of Literature and Amusement* of February 1844 shows that all were welcome at Chatsworth: "The Duke of Devonshire allows all persons whatsoever to see the mansion and grounds every day in the year, Sundays not excepted, from ten in the morning till five in the afternoon. The humblest individual is not only shown the whole, but the Duke has expressly ordered the waterworks to be played for everyone without exception. This is acting in the true spirit of great wealth and enlightened liberality; let us add, also, in the spirit of wisdom."

In 1849, the Midland Railway from Derby reached Rowsley, just three miles down the Derwent valley from the house, and eighty thousand people came to see Chatsworth during the summer. No charge was ever made until the ninth duke succeeded in 1908, when the resulting income was given to local hospitals. During the war, Chatsworth accommodated a girls' boarding school; afterwards it was opened once again to the public. In 1949, seventy-five thousand people came to Chatsworth despite the severe petrol rationing still in force; the charge for adults was half a crown (25p), and one shilling (5p) for the garden. For the first time the proceeds went towards its upkeep, and since then the entrance money paid by visitors has made a vital contribution to the maintenance of the house and estate.

Eric Oliver, Comptroller

Through the kind offices of the Duke of Devonshire I was put in touch with Eric Oliver, the recently retired comptroller, and Jim Link, the present head gardener. As I waited in the gatehouse to meet Eric, I was regally entertained by the gatekeeper: a cup of tea, many stories, it was like a man's home from home, apart from the closed-circuit television, complete with a microwave, a stove, a radio and the day's newspapers. But all these were needed by a man on a twelve-hour shift.

Eric led me through a labyrinth of corridors to the staff

sitting room, a rather grand room lined with leather-bound books. On the way a score of people asked him how he was, and enquired about his fishing and his golf. "That's how it is, you see," he said. "It's very much like being part of a big family here, even though I've been gone a couple of years or so.

"I was brought up at Chatsworth and I worked here for fifty years. At the very beginning I was apprentice house carpenter, though I had ambitions to be a gamekeeper — I've always regarded myself as a countryman. I never really had any other idea of what I would do apart from working at Chatsworth: my father had been the late duke's chauffeur, and my grandfather had been head gardener — he actually dropped dead pruning roses at the age of seventy-four! I suppose in many ways I'm very typical of many estate families, knowing exactly where to look for employment from generation to generation.

"One of my first jobs was to replace all the windows on the south front of the house. These had been picture windows, but the present duchess wanted to put them back to the original bar form. That is typical of the family, and certainly in my time every change has been thought about and considered.

"I suppose I must have done all right, because in 1963 I was promoted to house foreman, responsible for all the work that took place in the building itself. After that I became assistant comptroller and then, for the last seventeen years of my career, comptroller himself. The comptroller is responsible for everything to do with the house with the exception of the treasures. The administration was down to me, all matters of maintenance, staff matters . . . just about everything you could think of. Of course, the job has changed a fair bit in my time, most especially the problem of security. Fifty years ago there was just a night watchman whose main job was to wander around checking for leaks on a rainy night. Sadly things almost inevitably had to change, and now security is a big element of the job.

"Another element that's grown a great deal in the course of my service is the number of major occasions that take place in the park. The Chatsworth Horse Trials, for example, were a major headache. It was always a three-day event, and one of my many jobs was to persuade five farriers and five volunteer doctors to give up that amount of time. Then you'd be begging and borrowing four-wheel-drive vehicles from everywhere. It went international, of course, so I even had to concern myself with horse passports, would you believe! Then there were drug tests to take, and it got so involved that finally I was glad to give it up. And, I've got to say, horse people are not always the easiest to get along with!

"Then, of course, there were the game fairs that began to flourish after the war: it seemed at times that we just carried on breaking record after record. There've been angling fairs, county fairs . . . you name it, everybody wants to hold a fair in the park!

"One of my main problems being comptroller was the weight of the public presence. You must remember that well over one million people visit Chatsworth every year, so as well as the general wear and tear on the building, there is the problem of how to cope with such a pressure of human bodies. Most of the public are absolutely fine, but you do get some silly people from time to time. Once, I remember, we were even threatened with legal action because somebody had tripped over a stick in the park and missed an hour's work having to go to the doctor!

"Perhaps the daftest of all was the letter of complaint about all the dog droppings in the park. I actually went out there to see what the lady was on about, and really couldn't understand it at all. So I asked her to come, expenses paid, to the hall so that she could show me for herself, and it turned out that the droppings she disliked so much were from sheep!

"By and large though, we all get a great deal of pleasure from the number of visitors that come. You tend to find that you get relatives of people who had worked here, even a hundred years ago. I remember one letter from an American doctor who had an old Rolls-Royce. He had traced its history back to when it was new, and had been bought by the duke and driven to Chatsworth, way back in the twenties. I was actually able to send the man a picture of the car as it had been then, and he was so excited he came over to see us! I took him to the carriage house where the family cars were once all kept; the building is now a restaurant, but I do feel that he got a great deal from the occasion. I could show him records of all the Rolls-Royces the family has bought, way back to 1915; we've got the chassis numbers and the registration numbers of them all, right down to the present-day Bentleys.

"Okay, it's nice to close the house down at the end of the season, but after three or four weeks I always really did look forward to having the public back again. You see, Chatsworth really actively needs people. In the winter the house is dark and gloomy — then, come the summer, it's all chatter, light and sparkle. Of course, having the public in has always made it hard work for us, but there is a buzz to the place when they're there, that you never get when it's empty. There's no pleasing some, of course, but the vast majority are totally appreciative. I introduced the system of comment slips at the end of the public route, and we've had so few complaints that you'd hardly believe it. Moreover, there have been a lot of useful suggestions which we've always followed up. Of course, that's been the way here at Chatsworth from the beginning, the public having a right to their say.

"I like to think that we've always had a really high quality of visitor here, if you know what I mean; there's never been any vandalism of any sort, and no graffiti. I honestly do think that people are overawed as they walk into the Painted Hall, for example — you'll see them whispering as though they're in a cathedral. Of course, it's extremely grand, but they really do appreciate the splendour. What I've always been pleasantly surprised about is how little litter they leave: it just shows that if you offer the public a place that is clean and tidy, then they tend to respect it.

"As comptroller I was responsible for at least forty staff, and when the house opened, another fifty or so on top of that. I was fortunate that the staff turnover has always been very low: 99 per cent of people here stay for the duration, providing they behave themselves, which is fairly general. You tend to find that either people come and go very quickly, or once they have been here for a while they stay until they retire. The thing is, working at a place like Chatsworth is a most attractive way of life. Also, the staff are truly so well looked after that very few people want to leave. Okay, I've grown up here and you might say that I'm biased, but I have travelled a lot and I've never come across anywhere I'd rather live and work. The quality of life here is something special. In my old job, I used to go down to London once a month because I was responsible for the duke's London house. But, believe me, I just couldn't get out of the capital quick enough — I'd try and do everything within the day, and then get back home to the peace and quiet.

"I don't know what it is about living at a place like Chatsworth, but you somehow become an integral part of it. I regard this as my real home, and I'm attached to it in a way you wouldn't believe. Being a part of Chatsworth has given my life a special edge. Let's think back to when I was a carpenter: it was all quality then, not quantity like so many people have to live with today. There were no deadlines imposed on me. Every bit of work that I did just had to be first class, and that was the only criterion. There was no hounding, no chasing: it was just made clear to me that I was doing something for history. Mind you, I was very fortunate in learning from proper tradesmen, from really skilled people. Everything was done by hand and hardly any machinery was ever used. Tradesmen in those days never thought of retiring:

they just carried on doing the job they loved until they dropped and it was from people like this that I learned everything I knew. Standards are still maintained to this sort of level at Chatsworth today: everything that's done here has got to be the best, or it just won't do at all.

"I was very lucky as comptroller because I benefited from the financial improvements that began from the 1960s onwards. Money in the 1950s was incredibly tight, and it's good to see that all this has changed. Now the estate is truly viable, and this is all down to the present duke and duchess and their good management and their great ideas. I find it really pleasing to see the estate so vibrant again, really ticking along. Obviously, in my job I've been to all the major estates and I don't believe any are as tight as this one.

"You ask me what has been my most satisfying job? Well, possibly I'd say the restoration of the roof. Remember that this covers one-and-a-third acres! It's all lead, and no major work had taken place on it since 1938; it was clad like a quilt, and you wouldn't believe the number of leaks after a rainy night. We started twenty-five years ago on the roof repairs, and it was my ambition to get the whole lot completely re-leaded before I retired. I *just* did it, and the cost, believe it or not, was one-and-a-half million. We got no grant aid for that whatsoever because the duke insisted that Chatsworth should not be a further burden on the taxpayer, even though we could have got 40 per cent from the government. I know now that this roof will be sound for a hundred years, and I really feel that I've made a contribution to history in my own small way.

"Of course, I remember the grand occasions, too. For example, it was Chatsworth's tercentenary in 1993 — and what a time that was! We were all involved in the organisation. A play was written about the history of Chatsworth, and we built a stage on the riverbank where it could be enacted, with a stand for the audience. The house was floodlit, and there were firework displays and a feast was provided. The gardens and the woods were all illuminated, and it was a fantastic spectacle. It was almost like 1939, the first celebration that I can remember fully, for the coming-of-age party for the duke's brother William, who was later killed in World War II. I was eight years old, and I can still remember the marquees, the bands, the food, the fireworks, the droves of people . . . I've never seen so many people.

"For us as children it was always the Christmas parties here that were so special. There've always been Christmas parties at Chatsworth for the estate kids — tea, conjurers, entertainments of all sorts, and then the duke giving presents to all the children. The Christmas parties have always been wonderful occasions for the youngsters, and there are still nearly sixty children that come every Christmas. You know, I used to go to these parties as a child and then, in my days as comptroller, it was my duty to organise them! The Christmas parties were one of those occasions when I always had more helpers than I actually needed! But it wasn't always like that, I can tell you . . .!

"Chatsworth means the world to me, and I reckon that I'm one of the most fortunate men alive to have been a part of it. For example, at just twelve years old I began scoring for Chatsworth Cricket Club; then I began playing for the team when I was fourteen years of age, and I continued until I was forty-two.

"Talking about cricket puts me in mind of one of the characters here from years back, Bill Hadley, who was the estate lorry driver and used to take the tea to away matches. He was an horrendous driver, and it was just fortunate that there was very little traffic around in those days — though you must remember that he'd only driven a horse until late on in life when he was given this lorry. Perhaps one of his worst blunders was to break a stone gatepost by driving straight slap-bang into it. This was duly repaired and Bill was sent off to pick up the old one — and what did he do? Yes, he promptly drove into the new post and broke that one, too!

"If it's stories about our youth that you want, you'd be better to talk to Jim Link. We were friends all the way through our lives, and we're still very close today. I'll leave you with this thought about my job at Chatsworth: beneath the roof of the house there are 175 rooms, 3,426 feet of passages, 17 staircases and 359 doors. All this is lit by 2,084 light bulbs. There are 397 external window-frames, 62 internal window-frames, 5 roof lanterns, and 60 roof lights with a grand total of 7,873 panes of glass. I also had to consider the functioning of 27 baths, 55 wash hand-basins, 29 sinks and 56 lavatories! And that was just *part* of my job!"

Jim Link, Head Gardener

I was told that Jim Link was waiting for me up in the top garden, and it was his spaniel that first rushed forward to greet me. We settled on a bench amongst the roses, overlooking the house, the valley and the river, and Jim told me about his life at Chatsworth:

"Eric and I were brought up together and we always had the run of the park. Eric is three years older than me, and I always looked up to him as a sort of big brother. Everybody on the park thought of themselves as one large family, and childhood here was very special, I guess; certainly there were none of the worries that seem to afflict parents with children today. Everything was much safer, so rich in memories.

"You'd hardly believe some of the people that worked here when Eric and I were children. Tom Lord, the keeper, immediately comes to mind: he was a great big broad man who always wore a flat cap, and his language . . . you'd hardly believe it! If you knocked on his door and he tripped over his dog, then whoever was calling would get a right earful! Eric and I used to pick up during the winter shoots, and sometimes Tom's language wasn't even near decent — and you'd hear his voice singing out through the crisp dawns louder than the gunshot. 'Lord's in good voice today!' the Guns would say — and indeed, Tom didn't give a mind to what he said, whoever was shooting. He'd even use that sort of language to the duchess herself! He just had a whole set of rules to himself, that chap. One time he took his dog to Cruft's, down in London. He'd never been away from the estate, and hadn't a clue how to behave; apparently he went into 'the ladies' when it was time to relieve himself and got thrown out of the show by the security guards. I bet they got an earful as well!

"There were characters everywhere in those days — I remember the men in charge of the duct drainage, and especially the stone-wallers. They were good old boys. You didn't find them wearing jeans, but big, strong Derby trousers; and they had boots as big as rocking boats, and they went through tobacco like nothing. There was Jack Downs who always wore a pheasant feather to keep the flies off his head. He'd spit black twist tobacco around on the ground or you'd hear it hissing on his stove. He wore clogs, huge things, and he'd creosote the wood till they stank.

"I also remember Herbert Newton who worked in the forest. He had huge hands, and was truly a giant of a man. He lived by himself because his marriage hadn't quite worked out. He was always fond of his drink and was a real eight-pint-a-night man, but he lived to a great old age and he was very polite even though he was big and rough. I remember him coming across one of the ladies in Edensor who was spring-cleaning: 'Do what I do,' he said. 'I wait till a windy day and then I open the front door and the back door and just let the bugger blow through!'

"We kids were always in awe of these characters. We might be sent on errands to contact them or to take them lunch, and we'd walk miles and miles to find them. And you remember the clothing that we'd wear? We'd have wet corduroy trousers that smelt in the rain. We walked everywhere — there were no school runs for us in those days! I remember all us boys had our own sheath knife, and we'd all whittle wood. We'd make catapults — I remember Eric finding an old musket-ball maker, and we'd put those in the pults and you could even kill a pigeon.

"Us estate kids would form big gangs and we'd go out into the forest. We'd make shelters out of birch and light fires. We'd find old kettles and make ourselves tea, or toast a sandwich. We'd all be dying for a greatcoat, even though they weighed a ton when they got wet! I remember we'd put studs in our hobnail boots and see who could make the biggest sparks when we danced on the rocks. And we'd all try to tame up young jackdaws just out of their nest. We'd shout 'Jack!' and they'd come out of the trees and sit on the handlebars of our bicycles and we'd give them something to eat. Eventually they'd grow up and go back totally into the wild.

"Of course, we got up to tricks, but not nasty ones. For instance we'd invade local villages — you know, we'd blacken our faces with mud from the river and arm ourselves with stick bows and arrows. The trouble is, we'd get to the village and find it deserted, with nobody there! We'd tickle fish from the Derwent, too; Eric was brilliant at it. He would get his fingers under the stomach of the fish, and run them up and down from the gills to the tail — and suddenly it would be there, flopping around on the bank. We'd give it a crack on the head and try and cook it on one of our fires.

"I reckon the only thing we ever did that was remotely mischievous was during the war when the girls' school was here, Penrhos College. I remember we pulled the valves out of the girls' bike tyres. There was a hell of a stink about that and we all got into trouble — and rightly so! Policeman Roberts — 'Bobby' to us — was a local hero. He was stabbed in a pub in Baslow, and we just couldn't believe it! It was never heard of in those days, and our parents all gave us a good warning about the dangers of drink.

"I can remember the war to some extent, and I still feel spooky when I hear a siren going. I remember one day when planes were going down the valley, and I was waving to the pilots until I realised they were German Junkers zooming past! They began to shoot at the hall itself until they were destroyed by our aircraft a little further on. I know I ran back to the stableyard to take cover. Old Tom Froggart was actually mowing the grass around the hall with his horses and didn't hear any of the row up above . . . just carried on with his job as though nothing was going on at all. We used to have the local home guard here, and we'd try and pull their legs whenever we could. Their real name was 'Local Defence Volunteers' but we christened them 'Look, Duck and Vanish'!

"Then in 1947 we had that terrible winter. Chatsworth was really cut off in those days, and we couldn't get to Sheffield or Chesterfield for months. We'd been promised a trip to the pantomime as a treat, but it kept having to be postponed until well into April. I remember one of our horses died and we couldn't get it out of the yard for weeks.

"It was absolutely natural that I'd start working at Chatsworth as soon as I'd finished school, and in January 1950 I became a woodman. By 1981 I'd become deputy head gardener, and then in 1989 I became head gardener itself. I'm coming up to retirement now and I can't bear the thought, really. Where on earth do you go from here? Chatsworth has always been the hub of my life . . . you know, my mother always referred to 'our duchess', never '*the* duchess'. It was this sense of family, of being special, that I feel for the job as well.

"There are special places, you know, on Chatsworth estate: they're very quiet, and no vehicle's allowed into them. These are the sort of places where I love to come. I'm thinking of the Old Park, one place the public is kept out of. Here the deer have their young in the spring, and here they can find sanctuary during the big events. There are red deer and fallow, ducks and grebes on the pond, and foxes and badgers burrowing in the hillside. But it's the old trees that get to me the most. You know, in there the oaks are six hundred years old. To me, there's a real sense of history, and it's incredible to have a place like this left today. If a tree falls down we just leave it, and eventually it goes back to the earth; the insects invade it, and it provides shelter for the deer. Some people might say that fallen oak trees like this look untidy, but this is how the world once was before we came along to interfere with everything.

"I suppose a major part of my job, as I see it, is clearing out and replanting the woodlands; this is something I've done for generations. I've always realised that I won't see the benefit of it myself, but that just isn't the point: you know you are doing it for history, for those that come on after you. I've always been lucky to have had under me people who would get the job done — I've known what I wanted, and I've had the craftsmen who could carry the schemes out. All my woodmen have always been keen, all liked to see the big project going on. To them, like me, working at Chatsworth is not really a job at all — it's more like a way of life.

"I'll say this for the last time: Chatsworth gives you a very special way of life. I've brought up two children of my own at Edensor, and my parents lived there, both to a great age. You can go away, anywhere you care to name abroad, but you come back and you've never seen anything as special as Chatsworth is. You're proud of the place. You tend to boast about it, but it's something that means the world to all of us that live here. Chatsworth has been my life from a kid right through to retirement, and I can't ask for anything better than that."

Knebworth House

In the preparation of this book I received many a warm reply to my requests for help, but none more charming than that of Lord Cobbold of Knebworth House. Still, this only confirmed everything I'd heard of him. The following anecdote may give an idea of his character: as most of us know, Lord Cobbold initiated the great pop festivals in the grounds at Knebworth. Back in the seventies my greatest friend, Max, went to hear mega-band Led Zeppelin; apparently the music was everything everybody had flocked to hear, but Max found himself close to a man he guessed to be in his thirties calmly reading the *Financial Times*. Intrigued, Max moved closer, and in a lull in the music began a conversation, one which flowed very easily indeed. Soon it was revealed that the erudite reader was Lord Cobbold himself.

The whole family is well known for their philanthropic attitude. For instance, look at any family portrait of the Cobbolds and you will also see Danny and Harry Matovu, two boys who were taken in by them back in the mid-seventies and treated like their own sons; both have gone on to forge successful careers as a result of the family's support.

Knebworth House itself is somewhat more difficult to read. As Lord Cobbold himself writes: "The romantic exterior of Knebworth, with its turrets, domes and gargoyles silhouetted against the sky, does little to prepare the visitor for what to expect inside. The house has stood for many years longer than the nineteenth-century decoration would suggest, and the stucco hides from view a red-brick house dating back to Tudor times."

In the early nineteenth century it was a perfect Tudor house, but in 1810 Mrs Elizabeth Bulwer-Lytton, then the owner of the building, found it old fashioned and too large, and so demolished three sides of the quadrangle. The principal changes to the remaining wing were the concealment of the red brick by stucco, the Gothicising of the windows, and the addition of eight towers, battlements and a porch. Mrs Elizabeth's son was the famous novelist, Sir Edward Bulwer-Lytton; he succeeded her in the mid-1840s, and he wanted the house to stand as a Gothic palace with domes, turrets, gargoyles and stained glass. This remains largely the house that we see today.

The interior of the house has also changed over the years, many of the alterations being made early this century by the famous architect, Sir Edwin Lutyens, who married into the family. Sir Edwin and the wife of the second earl, Pamela, continued to work together for many years on alterations to both the house and the garden.

Finally, further mention must be made of Edward Bulwer-Lytton, the famous Victorian novelist. His study is maintained as he used it, as a testimony to the great man. Bulwer-Lytton was also known as a smoker of renown: "A pipe," he once wrote, "is a great soother — a pleasant comforter. Blue devils fly before its honest breath. It ripens the brain: it opens the heart, and the man who smokes, thinks like a sage and acts like a Samaritan." And certainly these characteristics have remained in the family to this day.

Patti Razey, Multi-Talented

I met Patti Razey in the Lytton Hall, a large building close to the house; she was in the throes of decorating it, to give it a Gothic feel. The hall is used by all manner of amateur dramatic organisations to stage plays and concerts. Patti was swinging from the ceiling, painting great Crusader-like flags amongst the beams. A wonderfully attractive, warm lady, she climbed down from her perch and began her story at once: "I was born in Yorkshire, and even as a girl decided I wanted to be a nanny. My idea was to forge a totally new life for myself and get to the United States, because I'd heard that English nannies were in great demand over there. However, I realised that it would be a good idea to get in a bit of practice first, and so I applied for the job here at Knebworth as soon as I saw it. Don't ask me why, but I was absolutely confident of succeeding, even though I'd got no previous experience whatsoever!

"I'd come from a very close family and, being young at the time, I expected to be quite homesick — but I never was, and I never have been: from the very first moment I walked into Knebworth, I've always been

73

made to feel one of the family. Also, there were au pairs around the place so I always had a close friend of my own age in those early days.

"When I first began, way back in May 1969, I was nanny to Richard Cobbold who was then just nine months old. Now he's in his thirties and, happily, I'm godmother to his own son. This is exactly the type of family we're talking about with the Cobbolds. In the first years, I lived in the house itself and I guess I had three or four different bedrooms. Now I live in the village, in one of the Cobbold houses; it is around five hundred years old and quite lovely. I do remember, way back in the beginning, always getting lost around the house. After what I came from, Knebworth just seemed absolutely massive with its four staircases and never-ending corridors. What I did find was that the job here kept me extraordinarily fit: babies here and babies there and flights of stairs everywhere! Remember, this was before anybody had thought about baby alarms, and I was always making the journey to the top floor where they lived and back down again. And if they weren't flitting around inside, then I'd be taking them for walks around the park, quite often with a stream of animals following me: I believe somewhere there's a photograph of me pushing a pram being followed by a baby deer and a lion cub!

"Of course, I grew to love the kids as my own, and I never wanted them to go away to boarding school. When they did, I'd go and visit them whenever I could — and I still have memories of sitting in places like Margate in the driving rain, trying to think how to entertain little Rosina.

"I suppose if I'd stayed in the north my life would have been very different indeed, and much less special. Living here I really feel as if I've lived my life on a kind of film set — though sometimes I have, quite literally: *Batman* was filmed here, and more recently *The Shooting Party*. The latter's cast and crew were here from October through to Christmas, and I became particularly attached to Dorothy Tutin. Then, of course, there's been all the glamour and excitement of the concerts here. Before the bands arrive there is the pell-mell activity of setting the whole thing up and dealing with the police. Talking about the past like this always makes me think of the seventies, especially. The Rolling Stones came here: they were lovely, and we became friends in a very short space of time. I saw Mick Jagger three times; the first time was to show him round the house and talk about all the treasures and the architecture and so on — he seemed to be fascinated, and certainly asked endless questions. I remember cooking him eggs and bacon for breakfast, and constantly finding him beers. The other thing that sticks in my mind is that he was always asking about the cricket result!

"Even though I wasn't officially chef at the time, everybody tends to muck in here at Knebworth, and during concert days I've cooked for the Beach Boys and, as I particularly remember, for Mr and Mrs Meatloaf: what a great couple they were! It seems to me that the earlier stars were somehow more friendly. They seemed more sure of themselves, more easy within themselves in some way; they'd walk easily amongst everyone, not really giving themselves airs and graces. For example, there was Pink Floyd, a great band and really talented, but thoroughly approachable and down to earth. I loved them all. Now, groups try to be grander in some way, but I put it down to a lack of security in themselves; they're somehow less sure of where they're going. However, we did have a lot of fun with Liam Gallagher of Oasis recently. He was pretty filthy after a couple of days at the concert and used the house for a bath and then wrote in the visitors' book: 'Clean again!' A nice lad.

"It's not just the glamour of the concerts and the film sets that's made life here so exciting: I've really just had my horizons broadened beyond recognition. For example, Lady Cobbold taught me how to ski. In those days we had an orange mini-bus called Lucy, and I would help drive it over to Switzerland or Austria in the winter months whilst the family sat in the back playing bridge! Then, once I could ski a bit, I'd go skiing in America with the family at Christmas. The family's always encouraged me to travel, and always given me support like that. I've been to Africa, to help decorate a house in Nairobi. Would an ordinary girl from Yorkshire have a passport nearly as fully stamped as mine, I often wonder? One of the first things that happened to me when I got here in the early seventies was I was taken on a flight down Knebworth High Street in a Tiger Moth with the estate agent of those days, Wing Commander Carr — see what I mean about life being different here? Then, of course, I've always had the use of the swimming pool and the tennis courts — in fact it's been one of my jobs to organise the tennis tournaments that take place throughout the summer. Everybody plays, family, guests, visitors, and it's all just great fun. Then there will be impromptu dinner parties, often with lords and ladies that I hardly think of as being titled these days, I've known them for so long. And sometimes, just when I think the day is all done, I'll get a 'phone call asking me to come to the hall to join in a game of charades, and then I'll be here till past midnight!

"Naturally, once the children went off to boarding school I either had to leave Knebworth — because, after all, there was no job left for me — or I had to diversify, and I'd so grown to love the family and the house that I chose the latter. You've seen me decorating here today — well, I've wallpapered around twenty-five rooms in the main hall and been responsible for many of the hangings on the four-poster beds. I started cooking for the family, and for their dinner parties, and went on a few courses to get myself up to standard. I've always sat down with them after the meal for a drink and a chat, and have always been treated as part of the family unless it's been a business meal or a formal dinner of some sort.

"I also went to college to do a typing course, and now I'm a part of the office team; in particular I arrange rotas within the hall. It's very important to have everywhere in the house covered, and there are always people dropping out for one reason or another. I find myself being very strict with the younger girls — for instance I won't allow any facial jewellery apart from earrings! Somehow that sort of thing just doesn't go with the atmosphere of the house.

"I suppose my daftest job, and my most short-lived one, was train driver! You know there's a small railway here in the park? Well, one day the train driver didn't turn up, so Lord Cobbold hoiked me from whatever I was doing at the time and gave me a quick lesson on how to drive it. Well, I took it out all right, but on the return journey I turned the braking wheel the wrong way and the train went faster and faster, straight towards a barn — straight off the track it went and into the gravel, and a crane was needed to lift it back and get it working again! Lord Cobbold printed a sweatshirt and put it on sale at the shop; it said: 'I drove the train off the rails at Knebworth!'

"See what I mean about fun! In about three weeks from now we'll all be going to their house in the Dordogne. I'll probably help drive there, and I'll cook for them while we're there. I'm looking forward to some hot summer days, relaxing and enjoying myself. See what I mean about things being different? Mind you, I remember in June a couple of years ago when it was freezing, and Lady Cobbold was out there sawing wood for the fire to keep us all warm!

"Yes, this family, this house have really been the very essence of all my adult life."

Derek Spencer, Head of Maintenance

Derek Spencer has been head of maintenance since 1970. He was born and bred in nearby Hitchin, and came to the house wondering if there would be enough work for him there. "Enough work for me!? I've never had a quiet day since. Within minutes of arriving I was moving the gamekeeper and then rebuilding the old forge down in the village. Then I had to move on to the riding stables, and I just wondered what on earth I'd done. You see, Lord Cobbold wanted to make the estate viable and he really was in a hurry to do so. He wanted to get people in, to show the public what a wonderful place Knebworth is. Knebworth really has changed since I arrived: now it never closes, it's always on the go.

"The festivals date back to 1974, and in those early days we didn't really have a clue. They were colossal things to put on. Total chaos. The traffic was unimaginable. We were all flying round like headless chickens. Then there was the litter afterwards — all that had to be cleared away before the park could be opened up to the public again. People just come here to enjoy themselves and to listen to the music but they don't think about the organisation with the police, the first-aid services and even the toilets. But you know, we've never had any trouble, which is remarkable when you consider that well over 125,000 people all gather here.

"We've managed to have a bit of fun along the way at the concerts, too: I remember an estate manager we had at the time, who must remain nameless because we liked to pull his leg a bit. Well, we had Bob Geldof and the Boomtown Rats performing, and we told the manager that at the start of the gig an aeroplane would come over and drop dead rats out onto the audience. He totally panicked, absolutely convinced that this was going to be part of the act and that we'd be contravening the Health and Safety regulations!

"The general weight of public visiting here is a problem. They're all very good, but the sheer numbers really do give me something of a headache. Of course, London is just on the doorstep and it's easy to get here up the A1 or the M1. All summer there seem to be rallies or special events, and just the general flow of people is huge. In 1971, when we first really opened, I remember we had just 12,000 visitors all year. That rose to 100,000 the next year, and it's been escalating ever since. Still, I think we all like it: it brings a real life and vigour to the place, and big houses like this one with their huge estates were really meant to be used and enjoyed by the people — at least, that's certainly how Lord Cobbold sees it. He loves the public to come and enjoy his home, and he really has a hands-on feel about it all.

"The old house is my major headache. Every winter, for example, I have real problems with the heating system. There are sixty rooms here, many of them enormous, and the boilers wheeze and the pipes creak and I just never know what's going to give out next. The gutters are also a problem in the winter; I don't know who designed them, but they're absolutely terrible during times of snow — if there's anything more than a dusting, you've just got to get up onto the battlements and physically throw it off. Otherwise the snow builds up, and when it melts it seeps through. I believe this has always been the case, for centuries. So it doesn't matter if it snows on a Sunday, a holiday, or on Christmas Day — then I just come into the park, get up there and get the job done.

"Probably the stucco is the greatest long-term problem of the lot. It might have looked a good idea at the time, but it's the sort of addition that leads to real problems. You see, the frost can easily get in behind it, and once cracks have been made, the water seeps in. This really has a disastrous effect on the brickwork behind, which itself is very old indeed. What I've done is to split the house up into sections, and each year I'll tackle another piece to try and renew the stucco and make sure that it's watertight. Really, treating an old house like this properly is a bit like painting the Forth Bridge: you never finish — you can never sit back and think your job's done.

"Mind you, working in a house like this is really not a chore, either, and you soon begin to love its fabric. I suppose my favourite room of all is the banqueting hall; some of the panelling there is extraordinary, I would say the best in the world, and there are times when I just stand there examining it, marvelling at it. I like to think back to the old times, what things were like at the hall. You know, your imagination can run riot when you walk through a house like this. This was especially the case in the old days, when the Cobbolds were always in London and the lights were out; then the place seemed to have an atmosphere all of its own.

"Now, however, there's a real glow of life around the old building. Times have changed so much, as I've already said. Lord Cobbold loves people around the house — family, friends, the general public; he sees everybody in such a positive light.

"I never really know what my job's going to entail from one year to the next; of course, the house makes its own demands, and then the Cobbolds themselves are always coming up with one good idea after another to keep me busy! I don't suppose I'll ever retire — I couldn't imagine a life without Knebworth and the constant challenges it throws at me.

"I'm a bit like Patti, you know. Sometimes we'll both meet in the winter, walking through the park when the public have gone and everything is quiet and the deer are all around, watching us from the trees. We totally realise that we've both led very special, privileged lives. Patti will probably be walking the dogs, thinking about a trip somewhere, and I'll just be musing on some problem back at the house. And then we'll be back, working away at our various jobs, me perhaps shovelling snow and Patti up to her elbows in washing-up water — both pretty menial, but that's the way life is, here at Knebworth, and I don't think either of us would swop it for anything."

Wacko Watkins, Forester

Wacko Watkins has been a forester on the Knebworth estate for over twenty-five years. We sat in the gardens as the afternoon drew to a close; the walls of Knebworth could be seen over the hedges, the evening light glinting on the remarkable façade.

"When I first came to Knebworth, Wing Commander Carr was the agent — and what a character he was! I think he'd been a bit of a rake in his time, but he was slowing down by those days. All the agents then used to be ex-military, men from the forces, so in fact they were just moving from one type of service to another. This type of agent used to represent their lordships in the true sense of the word, always putting the family's interests first. They were past the age when they were out to foster their own careers — the services had been their main career, after all; moreover they already had a pension, and a steady, secure lifestyle. This meant that they were content to live in the shadow of their lordships and simply do the very best they could for them.

"Nowadays, however, it seems to me that all this has changed. What you get now are younger men who are using estate agency as a stepping stone in their own careers. I suppose they perform well enough, given the conditions of the day, but they don't have the same long-term outlook as the older men who'd already had their careers.

"I suppose this type of change has happened everywhere. I remember when I first arrived that the head woodman was a stickler for punctuality — you'd never believe the precision that he'd work to. At 10am, for example, he'd knock off for precisely twenty minutes, to the dot. Then he'd have fifteen minutes in the afternoon, and so would you — and not a second more or less. And if you got into the yard ten minutes early at the end of the day you'd have to oil or sharpen some machinery to take you up to precisely 5pm, and only then you'd stop! Everything was done exactly to the clock, just as he'd learnt it from his boss before him.

"In those days, working in the woods was a more personal type of occupation. I often think that with mechanisation there's so much noise all the time that there's less time to think and to philosophise. You know,

83

in this day and age it's a great luxury to have peace; mechanisation has made the boring jobs in forestry easier, I suppose, but it's also meant that you lose a great deal by way of atmosphere, I think.

"Over the last quarter of a century you wouldn't believe the pleasure that I've had from this estate. I've had the freedom to roam, the freedom to run my own life, and I've had all this without the financial responsibility of shoring up the enormous edifice that is Knebworth. You can spend and spend, here — millions are needed to keep something as important as this going. But I just don't have that worry, and my duties are all enjoyable. Naturally enough there are certain problems with the job. Obviously the park is so open these days — and I'm not just talking about locals walking their dogs — so there are people everywhere. The whole place is honeycombed with footpaths, you know, and all this makes any outside work that much more difficult.

"This is a small estate nowadays, I suppose, and we all pull together — but that's how it's got to be with country houses in this modern day and age. Inevitably everyone fights his own corner as to how the money should be shared out, but the viability of an estate like this is too precarious to tolerate any internal bickering. We all appreciate that we're part of a greater whole, as it were, and so it's important to have a flexible attitude to the boundaries of your own responsibilities. It's no good standing on ceremony or saying that you don't do this, that or the other; everybody's got to muck in together to some extent. It's no good sulking, either — and anyway, you begin to realise that with a bit of patience and tolerance, everything comes round in its own turn. For example, I've had disagreements with head gardeners in the past about the need for a new haha. Sometimes the deer are difficult to keep out of the garden, but a head gardener hasn't realised this. Then he'll go, another one takes over, and you get the haha and the way you want it to look. There's no point in falling out over a problem, you just need to keep a sense of proportion and eventually things will fit together. There's no point in standing on principle, it's a question of coping and surviving, and as long as in the long term you all pull together, then you pull in the right direction.

"I wasn't born into estate service. I had been a plumber in Nottingham, but on the eve of my marriage I decided I needed a change of direction. So we got married on a Saturday, and I was here, beginning work, on the Sunday; our honeymoon was a night in a tent on the Derbyshire moors! My first job was directing the car park at eleven o'clock in the morning for an air display here, so you see what I mean about being flexible when it comes to country houses, even then. I had a new job and a new marriage and a totally new challenge, and my wife, who was a teacher, was also starting a new school. Obviously I took a big cut in money to be here, but it's all a question of lifestyle. To some extent I think that my wife pays for our life, and it's my job that gives it the style, if you know what I mean!

"We've loved it so much here at Knebworth that we've tried to share our pleasure; to this end we've sometimes 'borrowed' children, as it were — had surrogate sons to look after and keep out of mischief.

We've shown them everything that goes on in the house and the park, and I think that the experience has done them good: for example, one of them is going on to climb Everest in the army millennium team, and another has given up a high-powered job to become a nurseryman; I guess he'll be happier, and it is perhaps our lifestyle that has influenced his decision. If you ask me, it's not how many mobile phones you've got that keeps you happy: no, if you can kick the commercial pressure and live the values that an estate like this gives you, I think you'll be happier in the end.

"My life is wonderful here. I can wander round the woods to my heart's content, looking at everything going on, checking on the fences, exercising the dogs and thinking about the trees. I love that. Do you know, I like to think of the head gardeners in years gone past, sending their lads up the trees to trim the boughs so that we can see now. Of course, in those days they all believed that an old tree would be harvested to make a ship, and they would have laughed at the thought of iron boats, I'm sure!

"Trees: I love them. I've actually taken a tree to pieces, literally piece by piece. Yet if that tree had been put in a sawmill I wouldn't have had the time to study it and think about it; it would have been all noise and speed, and all I would have been worrying about would have been safety. But splitting up a tree by hand, quietly at home in the yard, gives you time to think; it gives you time to pay respects to the wonder of the tree itself, and those that 'groomed' it.

"People knew how to look after trees in the old days, and everything was done with a thought to the future. My first head forester, for example, was a manager for the future, I'd say. He was a hard man, but fair, and the cost was never the vital thing. Okay, he had to bear the price of everything in mind, but everything was still done in terms of quality and how it would last.

"Today, all that sort of thing has changed, and everything is sub-contracted and done to a price. The price has to be keen, and cheap — but, of course, this doesn't necessarily mean that you're going to get the best work done. When all work was done 'in house', so to speak, there was a proper overview of how things would turn out; but now contractors come in and just look at the end of the contract, and not towards two hundred years in the future.

"Take this morning, for example. I've been out clearing sweet chestnut, which I'll use for fencing, and it'll be fine for twenty-five years at least. To me, this is much better than buying in timber and worrying that it hasn't been dried or pressurised to the set requirements. I think this is being responsible. You select and fell and clear by hand, using your brain and your experience. I like working in a quiet, gentle environment, and I feel that if you use the woods wisely they'll repay you in every way.

"I've still got the tools that were given me by an old chestnut fencer years back. They're beautiful things, and although they're old, they've been well cared for and do the job marvellously. I still use them. These are tools that you couldn't buy today and I love to work with them. It reminds me of who I am, and what my role in life is all about.

"I believe strongly in coincidences, and I feel that, in some strange way, I was meant to come and work here. This is because in 1972 I saw an article in the plumbing and heating trade journal about the new boiler system that had been installed at Knebworth House. It was written by a certain L. W. Watkins — my own initials precisely! And in 1973, here I was myself! Coincidences make life interesting, but they help point your way as well."

Harewood House

I remember being taken to see Harewood House as a child, by my parents, when I was around seven or eight years old. My father was a north Yorkshireman but had worked as a solicitor in Leeds and obviously felt a great deal of pride in this nearby mansion. Returning to the place nearly forty years on, I found that I remembered much of the atmosphere. Of course, at that time I couldn't have told you anything about the architect, the landscape gardeners or the history of the family, but it is the spirit of these houses that is probably the most important issue. On a summer's afternoon in 1998, Harewood struck exactly the same response in me as it had done years before: somehow, its grandeur manages to remain friendly, accessible. Harewood is a place that could be daunting and remote, but somehow it manages to avoid this. Perhaps you sense that it is a family home — perhaps you appreciate the care that goes into the upkeep of the buildings and the gardens. It is as though you somehow pick up on the fact that this is a place loved and cherished by owners and servants alike.

Harewood itself is little more than a couple of centuries old, though the Lascelles family, who built it, had lived in the district for two hundred years before that. The magnificent interior was largely created by Robert Adam; it has superb ceilings and plasterwork, and it houses one of the finest collections of English and Italian painting in the country. There are also exquisite examples of Chippendale furniture, and extensive porcelain collections. The grounds were landscaped by Capability Brown, and are particularly famous for their lakeside and woodland walks.

The Earl of Harewood is the son of the late Princess Mary, daughter of King George V, and is therefore a cousin of Queen Elizabeth II. Princess Mary lived at Harewood for many years, and some of her pictures and possessions are still on display in her rooms. For most of this century this connection with royalty has been an important aspect of life at Harewood; certainly for those who have worked there it has given life an extra dimension, an added dignity, and none has felt this more acutely than the now-retired head gardener, Geoffrey Hall.

Geoffrey Hall, Head Gardener

Geoff Hall is one of the most charismatic men I have ever met. Is it his smile, or his deep, rich voice? His fund of stories or the twinkle still very definitely alive in the eyes of this eighty-something-year-old? Geoff's father was head gardener at Harewood before him, and Geoff himself has had a legendary influence on the gardens at Harewood, and their commercial development; however, here I wish to concentrate on Geoff's childhood at Harewood during World War I and through the twenties.

A recurring theme in my research was that childhood on an estate is quite different from the norm. Discipline and standards were definitely a part of it, but a vital ingredient appears to have been a sense of identity, a spirit of belonging that is so often absent in the larger, outside world. Everyone who has spent their childhood on a country estate speaks warmly of it. Perhaps this is nostalgia — but do we all remember our earliest years so fondly? This is especially so as we reach the end of the twentieth century and children are increasingly restricted and controlled in their way of life. Geoff Hall's childhood was not without duties, obligations and restrictions, but he still seems to have enjoyed a freedom that many of our children today would not know how to cope with. And perhaps it is this freedom from an early age that leads to self-reliance and the ability to see through problems for oneself . . .

"I was born in 1914 in the head gardener's house — my father had taken the position in 1912. I was about eight when my sister Margaret was elected from amongst Harewood school children to present a bouquet of flowers to Princess Mary as she and her husband, Viscount Lascelles, arrived at Harewood village soon after their marriage in London. I was one of the boys who had the honour of being chosen to pull the Rolls-Royce car by ropes down the mile-long carriage-way to Harewood House, where the couple were met by the fifth Earl of Harewood and his wife Florence. I well remember the occasion, because Lady Harewood had a dachshund dog that decided to take a nip at my ankle and for a little while all the main celebrations were forgotten and I was the centre of much ado and attention.

"It was about this period of my life that I had my first taste of horticulture. I was on holiday from school and wearing a pair of new trousers, and as I climbed my favourite conker tree I tore the backside out of them! I pleaded with my granny to do the necessary repairs before my father came home, but alas, it was too late for that. Not for me the usual one or two clips behind the ear or three or four on the bottom, but three days weeding the asparagus beds! Rough and ready justice was how it was in those days, and I was always up to some mischief or other around the estate. Very often my father would hand me his pocket knife and say, 'Here, go and cut one to suit yourself, lad!' There was a plantation of hazel bushes behind our house, and we had to select our own cane, a most ignominious task!

"As a young lad of about ten I would spend most of my time with the estate horseman, Dick Kettlewell. I can hear him now as he groomed Major, the heavy Shire, and Jack, the lighter horse we used for trap work. Not many of Dick Kettlewell's calibre are to be found today. You've got to realise that these men were extremely dedicated, practically born amongst boots and harnesses — though not saddles, because there wasn't much time for riding. No true horseman would retire for the night unless he knew his charges were properly fed, watered and bedded down — except in the summer months, when after the day's work the teams were turned out into the herds to graze until the following morning. The spring and late summer periods were arduous times for the farm horses, and both men and beasts would be on the move early: preparation for the day's work would have to be in hand soon after five-thirty in the morning in order to be ready for the manual workforce that started at seven o'clock.

"Many times I would rush from school and make straight for the potato field or wherever the horse was working, just so that I could ride or drive it back to the stable when work finished at five-thirty in the afternoon. I remember with much respect many of the twenty-odd gardeners that worked in the department, but Dick Kettlewell was the outstanding favourite. It was always a safe and sure thing that if ever I went missing my mother had only to ask father where Dick Kettlewell was working to know where I would be.

"Another of my stamping grounds as a child was the laundry — as you know, every major estate had one of its own, a gaunt, spacious-looking place. A dear old battle-axe whom we knew as Old Ann was in charge of ours, with Lydia the second-in-command; both were of Scots descent and with strong Quaker beliefs. The laundry lasses who worked with these old dears must have experienced a tedious, uninteresting and sheltered life because they were never allowed to mix with the local people in any form of social activity whatsoever. In part, the local lads were considered socially unworthy, a rough, rude, unruly lot! Then again, you've got to realise that in those days there was no really reliable form of birth control, and the last thing any housekeeper wanted was one of her lasses in the family way — life was difficult enough without any unnecessary complications! Woe betide any girl who did fall for a baby, especially if the father didn't come forward. The chances were that she would lose her position entirely and be sent back home, if the family would still take her in. All the laundresses wore clogs, I remember, which made a great clatter if work was in full progress. Every week on Saturday afternoon or Sunday morning, my sister and I would have to take some seasonal vegetables to the laundry, and we'd always bring back some treacle toffee and perhaps one or two magazines or journals that had been sent down from the House itself. Sometimes it might be a *Tatler* or a *Country Life*, and it would cause a family row as to who should have the first look!

"I was always hungry in those days, but there always seemed to be somebody who would provide me with an extra bit of food somewhere! For example, I'd make a habit of drifting down to the stable just before twelve o'clock and would wait until Dick Kettlewell came in with the horse because he'd always give me a piece of cold pasty from his lunchbox. Then I'd be off to the laundry where a dish of soup or sago pudding would generally come my way — and if I was still hungry, I would see if there was any milk to fetch from the dairy, for the dairymaids would always supply a cup of milk to drink on the spot! Only then would I move off for my lunch!

"Equally there always seemed to be somebody ready to give me a clip round the ear. I used to sing in the church choir, like most of the estate workers'children; I remember I was paid 2s 6d [12$\frac{1}{2}$p] annually, a princely wage, but I was always being pulled up by Canon Lascelles, a really strict disciplinarian. Then there was Mr Wadsworth the headmaster who used a cane even more than my father.

94

"When I was on holiday from school my father would see to it that I was kept out of mischief by giving me jobs of work; these were generally to do with gardening, pigs or poultry. It was customary in those days to have a household pig, and nearly every house had its own pigsty. A week or two before Christmas would be the time to kill it, and for some weeks after, meals would consist of pork, pig's trotters, pig's offal, or anything else connected with the sad animal, until everything except the bacon and the hams had been eaten. These were laid on stone shelves to await the local butcher who would do the necessary curing by applying salt and saltpetre to the meat; it was then left to pickle. Father's flock of one hundred hens, would keep me busy too; in fact I really enjoyed this work, and at one time thought very seriously of becoming a poultry farmer, so great was my interest in rearing chickens.

"I was only four when World War I ended, but I can still remember the bombs dropped from German Zeppelins; to this day there remains a depression in the church path where one of them fell. Two further bombs were dropped on the estate, one falling near Harewood House and the other on the clerk-of-works' house — this went through the roof of the toilet and actually landed in the water tank! I still remember sitting by the fire in the kitchen and listening to the drone of the engines above. Mr Deakin, the Harewood blacksmith, would always warn people of any imminent raid: he would cycle round the district telling everyone that Zeppelins were about, so then we had to get blacked out and show no lights. Old Ann and her staff would come up from the laundry to keep us company, and we'd sit by the fire with one candle flickering on the sideboard. Father would be relating some of his personal anecdotes to the laundry girls, but Old Ann was more concerned about keeping a firm grip on her bible!

"Although I was always out and about on the estate, I never got away with that much. I remember once coming back proudly with a swan's egg that I'd nicked from the nest when the adult birds were away. My father made me put it back, and this time the birds were in residence! That wasn't nearly as easy a job, let me tell you.

"In 1928, at the age of fourteen, I left school and started work under my father for a weekly wage of 10s 6d [52$\frac{1}{2}$p] — all of which I had to give to my mother. My starting status was that of 'crock lad': most large estates of that time would use thousands of clay pots each year, and each had to be crocked — this meant putting a few broken pieces of pot over the plant-pot hole at the base for drainage purposes. Hence the name 'crock lad'!

"The centre of everything in those days was the bothy, where the gardeners of varying experience were housed. Generally the squad would consist of one or two foremen, the first and second journeymen, and then all those still in their apprenticeships, called in those days 'improvers'. It really was a hub of activity. Each would take his turn to be the 'duty man', and this was a truly terrifying experience because for one full week practically the whole gardening department was your responsibility. You would get up at six o'clock in the morning, light the bothy fire and put the kettle on to boil, then be off at the double to do the rounds, especially if it was a cold frosty morning. First you had to stoke up the boilers and check on all the greenhouses, hoping that the thermometer in the tropical house was showing a reasonable reading; if it had dipped overnight there would be a real dressing-down by the foreman and then by the head gardener, particularly if the temperature had fallen to below the required minimum. Then you had to get back to the bothy to wake all the rest, make the tea and cook a breakfast that would have made Fanny Craddock weep, I tell you! I've seen some of the weirdest concoctions on breakfast plates ever to grace any table: bacon and eggs cooked by fantastic methods and served in most colours — mainly black.

"During the weekend further chores were thrust upon the poor duty man's shoulders: he'd have to fetch the milk from the home farm and sometimes deliver produce to the big house. He'd post letters for the head gardener who always seemed to do his correspondence on a Sunday; then perhaps he'd have to water plants if it was a hot summer's day . . . whatever was needed, the duty man would do it. Still, bothy life was a good thing for young men, creating a real comradeship and even brotherhood. As you can guess, there would be plenty of mischief, but there was no badness. Work and discipline there was in plenty, but very little pay: 34s [£1 70p] a week was considered tops, and if you wanted a holiday the same time had to be worked back as overtime.

"Of course, it helped if you were good at cricket! Then you'd be well in demand right the way through the summer. Estates in those days always had their cricket teams — especially up in Yorkshire which has always been cricket-mad — and generally the aristocracy would take some sort of part in the game; often the captain would be a lord, or a high-up official of the estate, and you had to be pretty good to keep your place in the team. However, a certain amount of animosity could creep in at times, particularly if the gentry had a friend to stay, or perhaps a lord's son would be home on holiday — then no doubt a regular would be dropped, or if playing, would be demoted in the batting order or not favoured to do any bowling. This happened to me once when I was on an estate and the three sons came home for the holidays; they did all the batting and all the bowling, and the opposition had a field day.

"They'd over two hundred runs for hardly any wickets, and the captain eventually threw the ball to me — after all, I had taken six wickets in the previous match! But I kicked the ball back to him and said, 'Not bloody likely, you do the bowling yourself!' Not only was this rude of me, but in those days it could have easily got me the sack — I was lucky to get away with it.

"Sport played a big part in our lives — that is, for those few hours a week we had a bit of time off. When I was a lad there was a very severe winter, and skating was in full swing on the 40-acre lake. I would take every opportunity to have a go, and I soon became pretty good, or at least I was one of those who managed to keep his feet. I would have half an hour's skating during my dinner break, and it was during one of these sessions that I was approached by the princess herself: she asked whether I would mind helping George who was skating for the first time — this was the present seventh earl, George Lascelles, and he would have been about eight years old. Of course, this suited me fine because it gave me a good excuse to be away from work for a spell!

"They were good times, those: I remember Lord Harewood arranging an ice-hockey match for one Saturday afternoon, and teams were selected from all those present. We had about sixteen players on each side. The princess was in goal on my side, and the sixth earl was in opposition. His lordship was an exceptionally good skater and never once did I see him fall on the ice, despite the attentions of one or two lads like myself who desperately tried to bring him down during the match.

"Before any skating could take place on the lake it would be my father's job to test the ice and make sure it was safe. Don't ask me why, but this seemed to be very typical on most estates, and you'd often find head gardeners talking about the job and comparing methods. Anyway, anyone caught on the ice before my father's declaration of safety would get a severe ticking-off. The testing of the ice was quite a performance. Father would muster about six gardeners of different weights and acquire a ladder with a hundred-foot rope attached. The lightest gardener, usually the garden lad — often me — would step on the ice and take the ladder, aeroplane-fashion, and push it forwards. All the other gardeners would then follow at twenty-foot intervals until the last man, the heaviest, would be well on the ice. Then at my father's command — who, incidentally, would be quite safe back on terra firma — everyone would have to jump up and down. Thank goodness the ladder and rope were never needed, even though I'm fairly sure Father had the situation well in hand because he knew the lake as well as he knew his right hand.

"A lot of responsibility came my father's way. Most large estates like Harewood would have their own fire brigade, and my father was the captain of ours for most of my young life. He would get the first call by telephone, and then it was his job to round up the rest of the firemen in his area; this meant a two-mile bicycle trip. On one particular occasion the fire was on one of the estate farms, and father received the alarm call at four-thirty in the morning. Off he went to his first call, Tom Baldwin the blacksmith: on arriving at the house he saw a light in the cowshed, and there was Tom, milking away. 'Come on, Tom, there's a fire!' he shouts. Tom just nodded and said he'd come once he'd finished milking. On went father to the plumber, George Baldwin, and after knocking on the door several times, up came the bedroom window and a voice shouted down, 'What the hell's up?' Father gave the instructions, whereupon George replied that he'd be soon on his way. Finally after getting the brigade mustered at the station, the team set off. The engine was drawn by the best of the farm horses, and after just a few hundred yards of galloping full tilt, the farm bailiff came tearing alongside shouting angrily at my father; in short, he didn't want the horses galloping and getting into a sweat. When the outfit finally arrived at its destination the farm was just smouldering charcoal!

"Estate life: yes, it wasn't all work, and there were many good times. For example, how I would look

100

forward to the big shooting parties that took place during my career as a garden lad. I relished the chance to go bush beating, and would be dismayed the times when my name was not on the list to go. Generally, three quarters of the whole estate staff would be assembled for the occasion. Each bush beater would be given his own package of sandwiches, and his drink which would be a bottle of cold tea. It was horrible stuff but it helped to wash down the dripping 'butties'! So long as you had a Woodbine cigarette to finish off the day, everything had gone satisfactorily!

"Once World War II had ended I was just delighted to come back to Harewood, the scene of so many happy memories for me. Of course, again it was work that dominated my life, but there was still such a great deal that was of interest and pleasure there for me. Princess Mary was still in residence, and I think it would be reasonable for me to say that outside the household staff I probably had more conversation with her than most. The princess would rarely miss her daily walk, a distance of nearly two miles, half circling the lake and returning to Harewood House. Her walk would follow a distinct pattern: in the afternoon she would be accompanied by her lady-in-waiting, but in the evening she would often be alone with her dogs. I could never really understand this, and it was my impression that our princess was sometimes quite lonely; I felt this on many occasions when I was at work in the summer evenings, and she would come along and just sit down and have a chat. Perhaps she would discuss the work in hand, or talk about some new plantings by the lakeside, and then both

101

of us would go along to assess the situation. Very often the royal lady would trail me back to Harewood House, which meant climbing a rather steep hill. I was fifteen years younger than the princess, but I can honestly say that it was Geoff Hall who did the puffing and blowing, and not the elderly lady when she said, 'Goodnight, Hall!'

"The princess was a tremendously generous, warm-spirited lady, and I think all of us on the estate cherish her memory very fondly to this day. When she died, I was detailed to take charge of all the floral arrangements at her funeral; this included receiving all the floral tributes, and displaying each in proper order as it arrived. Some of the great names from the Continent were on those tributes: the King of Norway, the King of Denmark, the King of Sweden, the Queen of Holland and the King of Belgium. Such tributes, right down to the tiny bunch of primroses from the not-so-well-off, made it clear just how widely she was loved and respected. Oh yes, the 27 March 1965 will always be a black day for the estate people here."

I took the photograph of Geoff Hall outside his house on the perimeter of the estate on a warm, sunny evening when the garden was streamed with light. Flowers, vegetables, rolling hills . . . it seemed so fitting that Geoff Hall should be back at Harewood where he so definitely belongs.

Frank Widdop, Butler

My second meeting at Harewood was with Frank Widdop, the butler at the house since 1978. Frank is in middle age, bright, bubbly, and very much the new breed of butler. Much like John Savill at Syon House, Frank does not come from a background of service but came to Harewood after a period in the Royal Navy. In his own words:

"I think you'll find a lot of ex-servicemen going into jobs like this, and I often compare my job here at Harewood as butler with running an admiral's mess. Certainly I had a great deal of experience of this sort of thing during my Navy days. For example, way back, lying off Gibraltar, I was looking after Harold Wilson and Marcia Williams during their negotiations with Ian Smith, leader of what was then called Rhodesia. I remember that we put Wilson into a really plush cabin, but Smith had to put up with something way down the scale! I think that a life in the Navy teaches you to get on with things, and to accept anything that a job can throw at you, and this is invaluable when it comes to butlering. For example, when the family are in residence — a time I always like — you can easily work sixty or seventy hours a week: that's nothing. But if they are away, then your hours can plummet dramatically, and twenty to thirty hours a week is probably the norm. But you just don't watch hours — it's simply not an issue. This again is like being in the Navy, in that the job is there to be done, and you just get on with it; it's all a matter of 'if and when' and 'give and take'.

"Occasionally I'll travel with the family to London, but most of my work is done up here in Yorkshire. I'll probably start at about six forty-five in the morning, just getting things ready and thinking about breakfast. Then

I'll work through to round about eleven-thirty, have a bit of lunch till about twelve or twelve-thirty. Then I'll be on again, with a short break through the afternoon, until dinner's over, which is generally about tennish but this depends greatly on the number of guests that are here to stay. I've got all sorts of jobs — I'll clean some silver perhaps, certainly wait at table and generally lead the team of housekeeper, cook and housemen.

"You could say that it helps that I'm married to the housekeeper! We live in the west wing; we've been there for twelve years and we love it — even though the steps are something of a nightmare. But then, our flat has four bedrooms with an absolutely spectacular view. I think it's good that we're attached to the house so intimately. The wife's jobs tend to include table service, ironing and looking after Lady Harewood's personal belongings. But we very much work as a team, and I'll help her just as she'll help me. We'll probably move when the time's right, but I'm quite sure that it will be to a cottage on the estate. It's become our life, you understand. For this reason I'll always work at the house, even when I retire, or so I hope.

"The houseman basically serves at table and does quite a lot of the cleaning. I suppose he does far more cleaning than I . . . but then again, I'm the boss and I've got to have *some* perks! We don't really socialise as a staff team — though I do genuinely think of us as a team. There will be an annual staff barbecue, but it's very difficult to fraternise with people under you, and then tell them off if there's a problem. I've always felt that you've got to keep things professional, and that very probably comes from my background in the Royal Navy.

"You get quite a turnaround of staff. A good number come into it not knowing what to expect and then leave shortly afterwards, not really happy with things. Then a lot of assistants we train up to know the job soon move on. What we like to do is take people with some sort of catering background, someone we can really teach. During my time here I've had ten housemen under me; the last one went to an MP's house in Oxfordshire, and a lot do go on to other jobs in service. Just a few opt out altogether because they decide it's not really the sort of thing they want.

"We've seen times change just in the period that we've been here at Harewood. Back in the late seventies, the heads of all the departments were called by their surnames, but now the fashion seems to be to use Christian names . . . though I'm still known by my surname, and like it. I get on very well, I like to think, with Lord Harewood, but I'm still employed by him: there will always be a gulf, and it really doesn't bother me to be known as 'Widdop'.

"I would say that we've always got on well with Lord and Lady Harewood. They are exceptionally special people, and will always find the time to discuss anything with you. I've personally been very satisfied throughout all my time here, and I would never, ever consider moving. I just couldn't say anything wrong about them, even if I wanted to.

"Of course, one bond that we have is the football. One of my duties — if you can really call it that! — is to take them both to Elland Road to watch Leeds United play. Of course, Lord Harewood has been the president of the club for many years. I'll also take him to test matches whenever they're up here at Headingley. This Leeds United connection has led to Howard Wilkinson coming here for dinner, and I do recall that he's particularly fond of pheasants. When Lord Harewood was head of the Football Association we used to go to the England matches as well. I suppose that's another part of butlering today — you find that you do a lot of general driving, whoever your boss might be.

"I feel I have grown close to Lord and Lady Harewood, partly perhaps because they've never entertained on what you might call a grand scale, and things are kept fairly intimate. They have a lot of family and many very close friends, so most dinner parties rarely number more than fourteen or fifteen or so. Both of them are very much into music and there's always a very civilised atmosphere here. Neither of them look their age, and they're both well and happy. I'd certainly be happy to serve Lord Harewood until my time is up, and I'll do anything I can for them — they've just been so good to both me and my wife.

"I have no doubt that butlers will go on well into the next century, even though the role changes constantly in slight ways. Probably a butler's life today is less formal — it's more about sorting out affairs for the people he works for. I feel that my job is not so much running a huge team as making life easier, ordering train tickets for example, just ironing things out through life.

"As far as I'm concerned, it's a lifestyle that is enjoyable and secure, and you can't say that about all jobs in this day and age. You've got to be sensible, of course, and you've got to be really trustworthy: that's vital. I've got the keys to every part of the house, and to the safe, too. You know, once upon a time butlers actually used to sleep outside the safes! Either that, or they'd put up a bed by the vaults. It's important, too, to maintain standards. Again, I really like my beer and my wine, but I'd never *think* of drinking on duty: that sort of thing is just not acceptable at all!

"Sometimes my wife and I go out, and in the early days especially, our friends used to ask me why I stayed. They'd point out that I'd earn a lot more in London working perhaps for industrialists or something like that. But I ask you, what good would that do us? What more could I get out of life than I do already? My life's interesting and I work in a very good atmosphere with people I'm tremendously fond of and towards whom I feel enormously loyal. I've never regretted spending a single day at Harewood, and that to me is the real test as to whether a man has enjoyed his life or not."

John Lister, Clerk of Work

I met John Lister, the recently retired clerk of work, in one of the old stables on the Harewood estate, recently renovated into a block ideal for corporate meetings, parties or even shooting lunches. He was admiring the way in which some of the old woodwork had been rescued and integrated with the overall, modern look.

107

It's very easy to think of life on the great estates as simply revolving around the titled families, a strictly people-orientated type of life, when in fact it is often the actual fabric and structure of these estates that is of more interest to those that understand them. From an early age Lister demonstrated this sort of bent, and a singular determination to achieve his objective:

"I was only a lad when I experienced a real setback. Mr Baldwin, the sexton of the church, had got me taking the ashes from the church boilers down to the old quarry, and the cart that I was transporting them in somehow got out of control. Anyway, in the resulting crash I lost my thumb. Everybody said that this would be a major problem to my becoming a joiner, and they tried to make me into a painter. But I was determined, and I stuck out to be what I wanted. It was a bad start all right, but I made it, and then lived my life doing exactly what I wanted.

"Mind you, I had the very best of help, and if we look back to the war years there were some great craftsmen, and they taught me everything I knew. For example, there was Mr Wilde the foreman: he was over sixty-five when I knew him, and he worked on into his seventies; he was responsible for the staircase that's now in existence, and the sash windows. He lived on until he was ninety-six, and you'd see him on his bicycle anywhere around the estate. He was also into boxing and teaching the sport, and on his ninetieth birthday the *Yorkshire Post* featured him thwacking into a punch ball! He loved to set out the elliptical arches that you see all around the village here. It's funny, but when I look at the structure of the houses or anything around the estate, that's when I tend to remember people from the past. When I began — and we're looking back over fifty years now — there were seven or eight joiners on the estate: Mr Pinch, and Archie Ambler who was the house carpenter, and Jack Baldwin the wheelwright, and altogether twenty-four on estate maintenance in those early days. When I became clerk of works there were still fifteen.

"All these men in one way or another managed to leave their mark. For example, Mr Brayshaw was the stone mason early on this century, and the stone heads that you see all over the estate were his work; there's one in front of the laundry. It's a similar case with the porches that were built, and the lovely estate walls; these were perfectly done with no joints whatsoever, rather like drystone walling. Over the last thirty or forty years cars and crashes have gone a long way to destroying this work, but it's still lovely to look at.

"For a craftsman like me, the best thing about working here is that you can appreciate the real quality of everything that you work with. Stone and wood I love — even though I'm a joiner, I love stone. It's a material that you have to carve and work with to understand. Harewood stone is a little soft, but when you understand it, it's got real character. Jimmy Woodburke was a great stone mason here, and people used to ask him whether his work would last a lifetime; and he'd look at them and laugh, and say, 'Aye, perhaps, — it'll certainly last mine!'

"We have a lot of Chippendale stuff here, and I was very lucky to be able to work with it as an apprentice around the time of the war. There was a back room to the joiners' shop, and that was full of beautiful things; I found them all fascinating. There were boxes of the stuff — gorgeous mirrors all allowed to go to rack and ruin, all sorts, but I helped with the restoration. So I was very fortunate in that I was as good as brought up with beautiful things. Mind you, so was Chippendale himself, and *he* was fortunate in the time that he inhabited because granted, he had the design, but there were also first-class tradesmen in London in those days — he had the material as well as the people who knew how to work it. Today you maybe have the designs but not the craftsmen to put them into effect.

"Mind you, my life hasn't always been dealing with the finer sort of things. I've made hayracks, trusses, even entire barns during my time here. I've always liked roofing — in fact anything to do with joinery. In 1947 we had a really terrible winter here, and the buildings were literally falling down. Set rooves were sagging everywhere, and I spent all summer putting up new trusses and rescuing one building after another.

"I think I really began to understand wood during that period. But I just love trees — I like to understand them, and I like to talk to old Geoff Hall who was the gardener here and knows absolutely everything there is to know about a tree itself. You know, that's the great thing about these estates, something that people tend to forget: I see them as oases of hardwood — ash, oak, beech and so on. The Forestry Commission simply plants more and more

110

softwood, and there's no real worth in it. That's where the estates come into their own and are so important. If you work on an estate with the sort of wood you can find here, you're into real joinery. I love walnut, mahogany, limewood, oak and rosewood. Hornbeam is attractive, and laburnum, too: that's a lovely wood, even though it's a bit hard. Still, all woods are worthwhile to my mind, if you treat them properly.

"Over the decades I've become very interested in how wood grows. And I know a lot now about the diseases in wood; death-watch beetle, for example — and I'm used to woodworm, all right! From loving wood like this it's easy to become fascinated with the craftsmen of the past, and for this reason the wood and the stone of Harewood have always fascinated me in their every respect. There's so much beauty here, so much understanding, and I'm just grateful to those great craftsmen of the past that taught me so much and helped to give me the most satisfying of lives."

Syon House

To be truthful, I wasn't quite sure what to make of Syon House. A great many of the country houses that I have visited have been comparatively remote places, situated amidst rolling acres and far from the beaten track of modern civilisation; whereas Syon House is an enclave within the M25, with the M4 just a couple of miles away, and traffic in and out of Heathrow constantly overhead, the jumbos lifting off every few minutes into the blue sky. There is a garden centre at Syon and a plethora of attractions; the car park is crammed, there are children chattering and shrieking everywhere; a dog barks angrily.

But all was not lost for me that day because I was to meet John Savill, a man of extraordinary perception and ability. When he met me, he took me past the façade of the house and round to the rear of the great building, which looks over the water meadows towards the River Thames. And suddenly we were in a completely different world: modern-day London with all its fret and bustle is forgotten, and as far as the eye can see there is a sublime vista of long grass, wild flowers and waving willow trees, with just a feeling of the river beyond that. Immediately you are transported back to a time when the

Percys of Syon would come from the capital by boat, progress across this wonderful, quintessentially English scene, and enter the house through what was then the front and main door.

John Savill is tall, straight and confident in manner, and you would never guess that he has just turned seventy: the mark of a naval upbringing is plain to see. At first I didn't think I liked Syon House, but John soon put that right! We entered the Great Hall where a lady selling guidebooks broke into instant smiles, and passed into the ante-room — John was not at all pleased about the state of the scagliola floor which, he believed, could have been better polished.

The dining room held fond memories for John, from times past when he had organised dinners and at one stage even did the serving himself; and he was obviously immensely proud of the Red Drawing Room, an extraordinary honey-pot of colours and treasures — the ceiling alone is remarkable, decorated with 239 medallions. On we went, with stories here, reminiscences there; and little by little the house began to live for me, and I began to see exactly why it glowed for John.

We entered the Long Gallery and he pointed my gaze up to the portrait medallions around the room; these show the lineage of the Percy family, which claims descent from Charlemagne, the first emperor of the Holy Roman Empire. He pointed out the medallion opposite the second fireplace: this depicted one of the most famous members of the Percy family, although he lived long before the family's association with Syon: Sir Henry Percy — the famous Harry Hotspur — was a son of the first Earl of Northumberland and the father of the second. He died at the Battle of Shrewsbury in 1403 and never succeeded to the title; and as every schoolboy and girl knows, he was later to be immortalised by Shakespeare in his play *Henry IV*.

There, too, is the ninth Earl, an English renaissance noble, friend to Sir Walter Raleigh, a man with a love of learning and books. There was a strong element of the Elizabethan adventurer in him, as his attachment to Raleigh proved; he also took his band of military retainers on at least two expeditions to the wars in the Low Countries. Later he was implicated in the Gunpowder Plot and was imprisoned in the Tower of London for seventeen years where, nevertheless, he used his time constructively: "He chose his diet, modified his apartments to his needs, improved the walks and garden within the Tower, administered his vast estate, read his library, reacquainted himself with Sir Walter Raleigh, and became an expert at shove ha'penny!"

And there is the first Duke of Northumberland, who took the name and arms of Percy in 1750 when he took possession of the house. He was one of Robert Adam's chief patrons, and engaged the architect soon after he returned from Italy. Adam drew up plans for the interior decoration of Syon House, and they were put into execution by a team of craftsmen and artists of Adam's choosing; though the costs were massive, the effects are magnificent, as can be clearly seen. The duke completed the transformation of Syon by commissioning a landscaped setting which, in the words of one of the great literary figures of the time, made Syon one of the "finest villas in Europe".

Lastly John pointed out the portrait of Hugh Algernon Percy, the tenth duke who lived from 1914 to 1988; and here, really, begins our story of Syon House as seen through the eyes of John Savill.

John Savill, House Manager

John's position has never been easy to describe: ostensibly he set out as a cross between housekeeper and butler, and he ended up as a type of manager. In fact practically everything that has gone on in and around Syon since World War II has been monitored by his virtually omnipotent eye. The important thing to realise about John Savill is that he was not born to this type of life. So often the people to whom I have talked have been from families that can trace their presence on particular estates back through very many years. But this is not the case with John, who was brought up in the East End of London and went to serve in the Navy as soon as he left school. He has, therefore, no inbuilt feelings of subservience towards, or even unquestioning respect for members of the aristocracy, and still sees them very clearly for the human beings they are — though, as he might say, human with a difference.

John still works at the house two to four times a week, often from 6pm to 2am. He remains a valuable part of the Syon team, welcoming corporate guests, showing them the treasures of the house, introducing new arrivals, and making sure that the catering goes without a hitch.

John came here fifty years ago subsequent to his engagement to his beautiful Barbara, who was offered a job in the kitchens at Syon after he had been demobbed. Very soon after, John himself was offered a job in the house, though at first he refused it: he was used to the sea and to travel, and he had very little patience with the idea of aristocracy. But Barbara pleaded with him to reconsider, and eventually he decided to try it for just a year or two.

John is as amazed as anyone that he is still here at Syon, enjoying his life, and devoted to the job and to the Percy family. To begin with he was part housekeeper and part house manager. After the war there was only a small staff, and new recruits were hard to get, but perhaps because of his naval training John was able to find people who were prepared to be adaptable. The implications of a job in service in these great houses had changed, and people had to be ready to turn their hand to all types of work. As far as Syon was concerned, there was no longer room for teams of specialists: the new philosophy was "make do and mend", and only this would keep the great house and the great family afloat.

Even so, when John first arrived in the 1950s he witnessed a quite extraordinary level of indulgence in the lifestyle at Syon House. Remember that between 1945 and 1950 Britain had been a largely lack-lustre country. The war took some getting over: rationing was still in evidence and these were grey days — but concomitant with John's arrival at Syon, the age of the large dinner party had begun to revive; in his own words:

"My first years at Syon offered me a sight of life that I'd seen only in films or read about in books, and which I found it hard to believe. Caterers were called in to prepare banquets; there were carved ice decorations of amazing intricacy and size, and food that any ordinary person had only ever dreamed of — quail, pheasants, dishes I'd never seen before, only heard about. And I still can hardly believe the huge amounts that were thrown away. I remember one waiter asking if my wife liked strawberries, and then giving me twenty-four punnets of them! And those huge ice sculptures were just tipped away into the Thames after use.

"It was all film-set stuff. The guests came in Rolls-Royces, there were dinner jackets and amazing ballgowns, and the chauffeurs often wore leggings; in fact it was my first real insight into the world of luxury. During that time I lived like a king: I drank the best wines and ate the best foods — caviar, even beluga, and as for champagne! Well, at Syon in those days you could almost take a bath in it!

"I have my own views about the people who work in these great country houses. You must remember that I don't come from a family of servants, from a background of service — but coming into this sort of life has made me realise that life on the outside world is never easy, and that these great houses, these great aristocratic families, are tantamount to a refuge for people who need sanctuary. In fact, working in houses like these is almost like being in the Services: you do your job, you get on with people, and you keep your nose clean, and providing you do all these sorts of things, then hopefully you're safe — you're fed, and these houses look after you . . . you might be on a par with the dog, perhaps, but at least you're safe.

"The Percys have always liked familiar faces, people around them whom they knew. What is interesting is that they are still a shy family. The old duke, Hugh, was a very private person and if you ask me, the staff could get away with murder. What the duke and his agents came to realise was that, after the war, it was hard to get replacements, largely because women, who would work for £15 a year all found in the late thirties, wanted £5 a week and no less. The war ushered in a new life for the working class, and they weren't going back to the times of 'yes sir', 'no madam'. In fact it was very hard to get staff on any basis, whatever their calibre.

"After the war, staffs all round the country were cut back, though here they were still pretty numerous. There would be lady's maids, and assistants to the lady's maids, and there'd be butlers, under-butlers, and footmen perhaps — and remember that all these servants would be looking after just two people, the duke and the duchess. Even the children would have nannies, nurses and governesses.

"It was an amazing life: the Percys' main seat is at Alnwick where they had a staff of twelve. There was a chauffeur, maids and a butler, and all these people would go back and forward according to the season. On 12 August, for example, it would be back up to Northumberland for the shooting season. All these people just to look after two aristocrats! You know, I often thought that the family of servants was more aristocratic than the aristocrats themselves! The housekeeper and butler ruled the roost: they knew their jobs — but in fact they knew very little else. Syon, the family, their job . . . that was all they wanted from life, and mostly they would have no other interest. Replacements who came on the staff would be very similar. I don't really like to say this, but generally they were never very bright. But you must also remember that we're talking about the early 1950s and we'd just had the first major Labour government. Wasn't it Bevan that said 'We are all masters now!'? Basically, the feeling was that Jack was as good as the king. This was a true wind of change. The in-servants only came because their meals were provided — the cook would even send up meals to them, to their bedsits somewhere up in the attic. The girls even had their rooms cleaned; they only had to do their jobs and nothing else. Take the average butler: he'd be given two suits of clothes, all his keep and his accommodation, and his pay was really little more than pocket money. No wonder so many of them were quite content.

"The Percys have always treated their staff exceptionally well. In the old days the staff would come down from Alnwick for three or three and a half months of the year, and a lot of them would complain about leaving their wives. As a result the duke built flats, here at Syon, where they could live. So let's take an average footman: he'd earn £350 a year, and he'd have a home back at Alnwick and a home here in Syon for the summer, so two houses on country estates, all kitted out with fridges and everything you could think of; these houses would be shut from August until May and used for no other purpose whatsoever. That's how it has always been with the Percys, in my recollection — just a very generous family. In sickness, too, you were always looked after: you were guaranteed your home and your wage, and there was no need for sick-notes or benefits.

"The people who worked at Syon during my early time were sometimes extraordinary. For example, the densest plumber ever worked here. The water supply came across the field in an old lead pipe, which was pretty well perished. Every week there was a leak, and the plumber just went along and dug until he found it. Instead of saying that all we really needed was a whole new pipe, he'd dig and spot-weld and fill the ditch up again. A week later he'd be doing the same thing all over again. This went on for two years, and you ought to have seen his time sheet! It would have paid for a new pipe over and over, and we would have had a constant water supply!

"The average servant wasn't that highly intelligent, though I hate to say it, because of course I'm a servant myself; but none of them really stood out. Everybody at Syon tended to be wrapped up in their own little world: food, clothing, what room they had . . . that was all that was really important for them. The butler in my early days, Fraser, now he does stand out for sheer nerve. He was an absolute alcoholic, and one of my duties at night was to go to the Angel and fetch him; the landlady there we called 'Auntie', and she'd ring to say when he needed picking up. He'd be as tight as a tick, and it would be my last job of the night to get him home. At first I had just a little car, and the kerfuffle to get him in was unbelievable! Sometimes I'd get him back to the house and would have to give him the fireman's lift to carry him upstairs; often this would be one o'clock in the morning! I'd put him into bed, and then next morning I'd call him at six; he'd have a pot of tea and half a tumbler of neat gin, and he'd shave, bathe, dress, call the duke at seven and prepare breakfast for nine-thirty. Then he'd totter back to his room blind drunk again. He'd just about get through his duties at dinner, and then he'd stagger back to the Angel and the whole process would repeat itself.

"Of course, all good things have to come to an end, and one day I was lugging furniture about and I put my back out; I couldn't move at all, and four chauffeurs who were visiting brought me into my room on a board — I even had to be hospitalised. Well, Fraser went to the Angel as usual after dinner, but had to get home himself; he tripped at the back door and banged his head, and fell into a coma. He died the next day. The old duke was really upset, and obviously felt he should have done something. However, very shortly afterwards there was a stock-take at Alnwick and they found that all the gin had gone! Seventy-two bottles of whisky were also empty, just filled with water to make it seem as though they were full!

"Then I remember Willie, a pleasant but pathetic steward! Fraser used to tell him to put his gloves on to serve dinner but when he ladled the soup into the bowls he would put his thumbs in and get the gloves stained. He was pigeon-toed as well and could hardly waddle, so there was soup everywhere, down dresses, down dinner jackets — you name it! You could always tell what Willie had eaten for breakfast as well because it would be spread up and down his jacket . . . nor would he ever change, and he would appear at dinner in just the same state. To make things worse, he couldn't count and he couldn't remember which of the guests he'd served. He'd also collect plates one by one rather than as a group, and minutes and *minutes* would pass. Fraser would be ready with the next course, dying to go to the Angel, and there would be Willie, still trying to figure things out! The duchess would just look on, shake her head sadly and say, 'Well, at least they're cheap!'.

"Then along came young Stewart. He was as green as grass when he came here, and with hardly anything to wear. So we fitted him out in suits, and actually took him to the British School of Motoring to learn to drive. We took him to deportment school, and really got him to look the part. And thank you very much, he said, and promptly left us to become butler to the Aga Khan! I believe now he's got a villa somewhere in the Mediterranean and is worth an absolute fortune!

"Really my life has become more and more commercially orientated here at Syon. By the 1960s it was clear that even the duke's money couldn't sustain the sort of dinner parties that we'd become used to: in short, Syon was in quite a desperate state and just had to be taken in hand. ICI came in with the duke, and they opened up Syon Park; they put in about a million, but they couldn't make it pay properly, not even with the first garden centre in the country, the conservatory and a pleasure dome. So they pulled out, and a bad period followed: the old duke wasn't really versed in business, and got into the wrong hands. He then tried to take on all the business himself and run it as a family concern. Fortunately, things got better from there.

"Syon has been used less and less as a dwelling for the family as the commercial interests have taken over. An older sister of the present duke lives in a flat with her two daughters. But more and more the house is used for commercial purposes, for public events, for weddings and even films. We've had some famous people, we've had some lovely people: I can think of Michael Caine, Sean Connery, John Goodman and Peter O'Toole. I remember when *The Avengers* took us over, and when another film-maker turned the conservatory into a jungle; everybody was dressed as teddy bears, and sweltered under the lights. We've had *The Antiques Roadshow* here on many occasions, and June Whitfield was just a lovely woman!

"That's really what my job is about now, making sure that, financially, Syon continues to do well in the future. However, I also feel a real need to help and serve the Percys themselves. They've always been marvellous people to me. They're a great family, with great wealth, but they've always lived simply and now, especially, they have no grand cars or clothing and there's no real opulence in the house. The furniture, after all, has been handed down father to son over the generations; it's all listed and all kept in perfect state. The Percys today eat the food of the simplest kind — in fact I've often thought, especially in the past, that they went out in order to get a good dinner!

"Once your loyalty was proved to this family, you were taken in and they wouldn't worry about what they said or did in front of you, assuming that whatever you heard you wouldn't tell because you respected it was their business and not yours. In fact, tittle-tattle has always been discouraged here. Elder statesmen, like a good butler, have always put servants in their place.

"I've seen the attitude of the family change between the 1950s and the 1990s. I believe they've realised more and more that their concept of the world is — certainly was — actually different to how it is. The old duke, bless him, took it on himself to see how the world was, and moved out of his pampered circle into one which was completely unknown to him. Remember, at Alnwick he was known as the King of Northumberland; but he learned to knock on the door of his farmers, have a whisky, and listen to their complaints. Before this, everything had gone on through the agent; but the old duke thought things through and tried hard to see what made people tick.

"Mind you, there was still the aristocrat about him: for example, I might put the things out for breakfast, but he would just sit there and sit there and not even boil the kettle if I failed to appear for any reason. The new duke, on the other hand, is a part of the modern world: he will drive himself, apart from on special occasions, and he will beg a lift to the airport like anyone else.

"I've got so much to be thankful to the Percys for. Think of my younger son, Peter. He's got a good law degree now and is part of a successful practice, and this was all thanks to the old duke. The old duke particularly appreciated my wife, and when she died, he said that he would help with Peter; and he was as good as his word, contributing to his university fees, something I really couldn't have managed without him. Then when the old duke died, Harry, the eleventh duke, took over the payments without even a murmur. God bless him for that. People often used to ask me why I stayed on in service like this, but a life here is different. Most employers are pretty ruthless, but here, even if a person becomes surplus to requirements, they're not cast off into the world. Look at the house I live in now: it's rate free until I die. I feel it is a very great privilege indeed just to be here.

"It was one of the saddest times of my life when the old duke died. He'd been driven down from Alnwick on a dreadful night, and when he came in he didn't want any food, which was unusual for him. He went to bed early, and it was me that found him dead in the morning. It was terrible for me. All I could remember were the times that he'd invite me into his study at Syon, pour out a whisky or a sherry perhaps and we'd talk about the events of the day.

"Things didn't improve much for the Percys when Harry took over. Now, everybody knows that he suffered from ME. But he was a sad figure, weighing up to nineteen stone but wanting to live the image of a playboy — he felt he should go out with glamour girls, but really he was living on the doctor's prescriptions.

"I found Harry dead in the same room as his father had died in, and I felt just horrible about it. The Percys are entitled to be buried in Westminster Abbey but their crypt is now full, and I had to go up to Alnwick for Harry's funeral. There were representatives from Syon, and the Alnwick staff entertained me afterwards. I stayed up there for seven days, but it was a very, very sad occasion.

"Syon and the Percys have cared for me for forty-five years. I've had a good job in a great house, and that has been true for my wife and children, too. But in my view, aristocrats have got to be a dying breed, really. There are many new recently rich people who try to come up to that level — lots of wealthy people try — but they don't have the shine, and I repeat that word, *shine*, of the genuine aristocrat. It sounds terrible when I think of my background, but that's what I think now. There is something definitely special about the Percys.

"Mind you, their style of life is dying out. The present duke has no side whatsoever, and you'll find him in a crumpled suit just sitting reading the paper like an ordinary man. The duchess is beautiful, but she's the same: she drives a normal car, and leads a normal life, and takes her kids out to all the normal sorts of places. You know, the old duke would have had a fit if he could have seen it all; now there's no cook, no chauffeur, no butler or anything like that. I've moved from being a personal servant into more of a corporation man, but whichever role it's been, this has always been more a vocation than a job. It's never been a nine to five, and you can forget that type of lifestyle if you want to go into service. You give your life over, to a large extent; there are no weekends any more for you, and you give up all your social life.

"My life really has run with the Percys. I've shared their happinesses and their tragedies, and when there's been time for a celebration, I've often shared champagne with them — very often because Fraser was too drunk to pour it himself, and I said that I'd serve it for them! Certainly when the old duke died I was heartbroken, as I was when Harry followed him.

"I've always felt a friend to them, not just an employee. When I lost Barbara, my dearest wife, I lost track to some extent but the family helped me back to reality.

"I'm really surprised that I could feel all this for my employers. At the end of the war my attitude was just like that of all service men, and I'd have said that it was our turn to do the grinding — but that's not how it's been, and it's always been a give-and-take sort of relationship here: if you did your job well and were trustworthy, then the Percys would always look after you. And whatever happened, there'd be no song and dance. I remember the old duke looking after staff who had cancer, or breakdowns or whatever, and there was never any fuss made about this, he just did it out of the goodness of his heart. You can't help but like and respect people like that."

Before I left, John asked me if I'd like to share a glass of champagne with him. The cork popped loudly in the kitchen and he brought two flutes bubbling to the brim. "You know, this champagne — and I have some most days — is thanks to the old duke who took out a personal pension for me. That's how I come to enjoy champagne every day of my life if I want it — sitting here, in this wonderful house, overlooking the water meadows to the Thames.

"One amusing point I remember: it was always the case that house staff were called by their surnames, but here, I was always addressed as John. I really thought that was nice, and I said as much one day to Her Grace. She looked surprised, and replied, 'That's simple, John — we don't know your surname!'"

Caer Beris Manor

Caer Beris Manor is situated in Builth Wells, deep in mid-Wales; it is yet another example of a fine country house that has had to change identity in order to survive the modern age. Today it is a charming country house hotel run by its owners, Peter and Catherine Smith; only thirty years ago, however, it was the family seat of Lord Swansea and one of the grandest homes in Wales.

Caer Beris is dramatic in its setting. Although there is no record of a dwelling house on the site before 1896, there is strong evidence of an ancient fortification dating back to Roman times: indeed, the meaning of the name is the fort, or the camp, of Peris — or Beris — who is believed to have been an old Welsh prince. Fortification was of the motte and bailey type, though the only visible evidence of this is a large circular mound with oak trees growing upon it, on the right of the drive at the approach to the house. The site is clearly suitable as a stronghold: perched on high ground, it is almost surrounded by the River Irfon, a major tributary of the Wye, and commands extensive views of the surrounding countryside.

The building of Caer Beris was started in 1896 by local dignitary, Mr Harcourt Wood, and was completing in 1911. The house is timbered throughout in elm with plastered brick in-filling. It is roughly U-shaped, the principal rooms lying in the central portion. Originally the south wing contained the gracious family rooms — the billiard room, the dining room and the sitting room, for example; these are now the principal hotel rooms, overlooking the grounds and the river. The north wing, formerly servants' and nursery quarters, now contains the kitchens and bedrooms. In 1923 Caer Beris Manor was bought by the third Lord Swansea, and it remained in the family for nearly the next half century. It is towards the end of the period that Rose and Jimmy Price worked for the Swansea family, a period they remember with great affection. Today they live in a bright, comfortable bungalow on the outskirts of the town. They still have a view of the house, with the River Wye curling its way towards England and sea.

Rose Price, Nursery Maid

"I began working for Lord and Lady Swansea in 1957 as nanny to their son Richard, who was then five months old," Rose began. "Less than a year later Amanda, his sister, was born, so for my time there I had the two children to look after. I began looking after children at the age of sixteen as a nursery maid, and worked for the Countess of Plymouth in Ludlow. I remember that I never applied for the job, but that the Swansea family heard of me through friends and invited me to take up the position.

"Caer Beris was lovely in those days, a real family home and not too grand. There were three girls working in the house full time: me, Elaine the cook and Sheila the housemaid. There were two gardeners and a boy outside, and later on, Jimmy came to work here as well; several people came in on a daily basis, too. There were cleaners, and when large parties were held, local women were called in to wait at tables; the gardener's wife, for example, would help out. There was also a whole string of au pairs, German girls mostly, and Spanish and Italian lads would be taken in to learn the language and give some general help around the place; a lot of them did some cooking as well. As nanny, though, my job was just to look after the children, though I did do quite a deal of sewing, both for Lady Swansea and making the children's clothes.

"My days were really full. I'd be up at about seven thirty in the morning, and a tray with all our breakfasts would arrive up from the kitchen beneath. I'd clear the nursery table and get the breakfast set out, and then wake the children and dress them. Lord and Lady Swansea might well pop in then, just to say good morning to them. From that moment on I was on my own with the children all day long. They were never allowed to go outside by themselves in the grounds; it was just too dangerous with the river winding its way so close. During the day when they were babies it took most of my time just to keep them clean, and I'd also do their washing and ironing. Sometimes I'd get a bit of a break when I put them in their pram to have a sleep.

"After lunch we always took a walk outside in the grounds, whatever the weather; this was the case every day of the year, including Christmas. We'd take tea in the nursery, and that was when Lady Swansea would often join us. After tea I'd take the children down to the smoking room, which is now the bar in the hotel, and I'd leave them there with their parents for about an hour. Then I'd be called to bring them up and put them to bed. As babies, they were always in my room — in fact I never had a room of my own all the time that I was at Caer Beris.

"All our rooms were very attractive. The day nursery was over the front door, so we could see everything that was happening in the courtyard beneath. There was a rocking horse and a playpen and a huge cupboard full of toys; there were two armchairs and a sofa and a really thick pile carpet, and a lovely fireplace. We used a lot of the old Swansea china, never realising just how valuable it was. Everything there was antique, probably worth a fortune, and it was all tremendously cosy, especially in the winter. The night nursery was next door to the day room. There was a bathroom, and then my own room, which was over the kitchens. There was a tiny nursery kitchen with a sink and a fridge — no cooker or anything like that, because we always had our meals sent up.

"Looking back, I realise we had *lots* of fun, and I have very fond memories of those times. At one stage we had a donkey and a trap: the donkey was called Wellington and we'd harness him up and go down the drive, out of the gate and along the road towards the golf club. When Wellington had had enough he would just sit down — he'd put his bum on the road and wouldn't budge another step! Jimmy and I were getting to know each other by then and though I wasn't strictly supposed to see him when I had the children with me, sometimes the temptation was just too much and I'd bundle them into the trap and we'd set off to his house in Western Grove. It was Wellington that nearly gave me away once. Lady Swansea took him out without my knowledge and came back *very* puzzled . . . 'Why did Wellington make straight to Western Grove and stop outside No 14?' she asked me! Well, I said I just couldn't think . . . !

"We'd go out quite a lot. The Swansea children weren't allowed to play with the local boys and girls, so we'd arrange parties either at Caer Beris or in other large houses. Christmases were fun, too, and there was always a great big house party; other children would come along with their nannies, and the nursery would be just vibrating with life. Lord Swansea's sister had two children, and they'd always be there with their nanny. There'd be too many of us up in the nursery to go down to the dining room and join in the main party, so we'd all get on with it and have great fun by ourselves!

"Obviously I couldn't have very much time off at all because my job was so demanding, but even so, we really had some lovely times at Caer Beris in those days. You see, we were all youngsters together, all with boyfriends — the local lads would call the drive up to the house the Golden Mile! The Swanseas were really generous about all this, and Lady Swansea would always tell us if they were going out and ask us to invite our boyfriends round. Often they'd give us a bottle of wine, and if Jimmy appeared he was always made welcome.

"As the children grew up, I would take them on holiday. Sometimes we'd take the Swanseas' huge caravan, on other occasions we'd actually rent a cottage — and we'd always take a cook with us! Sometimes we'd go by train, other times we'd be driven by Old Man Malt, who had been the chauffeur and became the ancient retainer! We never travelled with the Swanseas, though, even if we were going in the same direction! They might put us on the train and then travel there separately by car!

"I really loved those children. When Amanda was eight it was me and Jimmy that drove her down to boarding school; she looked so tiny walking in through the great door, and then she looked back and waved to us. She was quite happy about the whole thing, but on the way home both Jimmy and I were in tears: it really seemed like an end to an era.

"I was paid £4 a week at the time, though I think it probably went up to £5 right at the end. This was pretty good pay in those days because I was living in and all my food was provided. The housemaid, for example, only earned £2 a week, and even that was considered quite decent.

"I always felt very much part of the family — and I might even be centre stage, as at Amanda's christening, for instance, when I was surrounded by bishops and lords! Much later both Jimmy and I went to her wedding, too. Even though I had children of my own, both Amanda and Richard were always very special to me — and they still are. Over those years I always had a really good relationship with Lady Swansea, too; some people found her a bit difficult and volatile, but not me. But then again, I suppose she realised how important I was to them! Lord Swansea, by way of contrast, was very placid, very quiet.

"I was often at Caer Beris on my own. Lord Swansea was into shooting in a big way, and spent a great deal of his time at Bisley; he was a captain of the British Rifle Association — he won a gold medal at the Empire Games — and this meant that he was away at Bisley for anything up to six weeks in the summer. Then they'd both be off up to Scotland for the deer stalking and for the grouse and pheasant shooting. They would also go to London, of course, since he was a member of the House of Lords, and I think Lady Swansea loved to get out of Wales and enjoy the high life. Even though I was on my own so much with the children I never once felt frightened at Caer Beris. People talk about old houses being haunted, but I never felt anything strange there. There was a labrador and a spaniel there with me, and it was just such a homely, warm place. I remember one particular time when I was much more frightened of one of the Spanish boys! I didn't trust him at all, the way he looked at me, and I made sure a lock was put on my door! Then Jimmy and I got married . . ."

Jimmy Price, Maintenance Man

"When Rose and I got married," Jimmy said, "I was offered a job as the general maintenance man around the estate; we needed a home and the stable house came with the job, so I took it. I was groom, groundsman, chauffeur — you name it, I would do it — and it sometimes seemed there was no end to my duties. I even did a bit of game-keeping from time to time, because Lord Swansea was such a great shot and always put a couple of hundred pheasants down on the land around the house.

"Of course, I was a young lad and at that time I hadn't really gone out of the county; you just didn't travel nearly as much in those days. And there I was driving this huge car around! At first they had an Austin Princess, and then a Humber Imperial which we brought back from the London Motor Show — that was a grand car, with automatic transmission, which was highly unusual in those days. So there I was, just a kid really, driving the Swanseas everywhere — to Bisley, London, you name it! And when we got home Rose and I would have to get onto the motorbike and sidecar!

"All this was a new world to me, because obviously I'd never ever mixed with the aristocracy; and they were quite a different sort of people to any I'd ever met before. For example, you'd take Lord Swansea to a station, and find he hadn't any money because they never carried any cash around at all. I'd end up, often as not, lending them 10s so they could buy themselves a meal before the train went! It was like being in a world apart. Or then I'd get a 'phone call from them saying they were leaving Scotland, and telling me to pick them up at Shrewsbury. They'd add that they were bringing a couple of stags with them, and so I'd have to go up there in the Land Rover to fit everybody in!

"It was all very glamorous. I remember driving Lord Swansea to Bisley one year when the Sultan of Brunei and his sons, the princes, were visiting. I remember the princes were dressed up all in Beatle gear! Lord Swansea, as captain of the club, showed the sultan round and then led him to the club-house for lunch. All the gentry were in one part of the club house and we chauffeurs were in another. Well, all the food was taken in to the gentry first, and then everything that was left — which was a lot, I'll tell you — was brought in to us. I'd never seen food like it in my life. Salmon vol-au-vents! I'd never even guessed that people could live like this!

"I also helped a great deal in the gardens. In those days they were an absolute picture, really beautiful. All the lawns were cut right down to the river and all the way along the drive; the gardener and I used to mow the grass and it would take us three full days to cut. And then we had to cut all the walks through the woods, and we had to do this with scythes because we had no electric tools in those days. The hedges up the drive were also immaculate, always clipped to perfection; we would shape great big orbs on top every few yards to give a really dramatic effect. Oh yes, the gardens were brilliant in those days, truly breath-taking.

"One of my jobs was to light the Aga in the kitchen every morning for the cook. In particular I liked this task at Christmas, because I for one had just never seen anything like the food that would be laid out in the kitchens. Everything was on such a vast scale! There were whole salmon, huge things, and I'd help the cook lift them out of the fish kettles, and the turkeys were massive as well. Everything was decorated, and the dining room was made to look really dramatic. Even now I can remember the sights and the smells — it was a time of incredible celebration.

"Everything then was home grown, and I'd bring peaches, strawberries, peas, carrots, onions, potatoes — anything and everything that was then in season — from the walled garden. I'd have my instructions and go up there with a basket and bring it back fresh. What we didn't eat at the time would be put in huge freezers to keep us going through the winter.

"We even had our own trout. Over the river, across the swing bridge, is the lake which in those days Lord Swansea owned. Well, he'd catch trout and then put them in a deep well that was fed by the overflow stream, and then whenever trout were needed by the kitchen I'd just go to the well and scoop them out! Those were the days, too, when there was salmon a-plenty in the river, and the estate owned miles of prime beats. You'd go down in the autumn and see salmon after salmon just ploughing up the falls, and then you'd see them pressed together on the spawning beds like sardines in a can, thousands of them. Sometimes Rose and I would go for a walk and watch them for ages, pressed in the fast water looking for oxygen, I guess. Lord Swansea would have his salmon rods made up all the time on the walls outside, underneath the billiard room, so that he could get down to one of the pools at a minute's notice.

"There was never really any end to my duties at all, and even though, on paper, I was only supposed to work from eight o'clock in the morning till five o'clock in the evening, it was never like that. Whenever there was an emergency I was expected to step in and help sort it out. Rose will certainly remember the time of the central-heating disaster! In those days the heating was with cast-iron pipes and radiators. Old Mr Malt — who had lived in the stable house and who was now in the big house — was in charge of the boiler. Even though he was seventy-five or even eighty, believe it or not he was courting again! Anyway, one night in the middle of winter he decided to stay out with his girlfriend! Well, it was freezing that night, the boiler went out, and the whole system froze solid for two days. When the thaw was forecast, old Mr Malt and I sat up waiting . . . and at around midnight the air began to warm up. There was a lot of creaking and groaning, and then the water began to spill through from the attic, sprinkling through the bedrooms and into the sitting rooms. We did what we could, but the water got onto the furniture everywhere, lifting the veneers and staining all the carpets. The whole house had to be redecorated, and a lot of the furniture was sent down to London for renovation. In some ways this disaster was a good thing, because the house had been getting quite run down even before it sustained such damage; a contributory factor was that the army had had it during the war — the officers had lived in it — and a lot more of the house had been shut up.

"I was a mad keen footballer in those days, but I could never guarantee that I'd make it to the match on time! The Swanseas had a lot of garden parties, and I was always 'volunteered' to give the children rides in Wellington's cart! I remember one afternoon it was getting near three o'clock kick-off time and I couldn't get the donkey and cart back up to the stables! Wellington was doing his digging-in act and just wouldn't budge. I remember taking the cart off him and pulling it up to the stables myself because that was the only way I could get Wellington up there! Yes, you name it and Jimmy would be asked to do it.

"Best of all I enjoyed my work as groom. I'd always loved horses, and when I accepted the job at Caer Beris I was sent away for a couple of months' training. We ran a stud here in those days, and people used to bring their mares to our stallion from all around. There were about forty horses altogether, and we'd go to all the agricultural shows with our Welsh ponies. I loved all that. We'd meet fascinating people and often be the stars of the whole show!

"My own favourite was our stallion, a really fantastic character called Siglen Las. I hadn't been here long before he had strangles, a glandular infection which can erupt in the wind-pipe. I nursed him for a full three or four months down in the stables and he became really tame. My normal routine during the week was that I'd feed all the horses early in the morning; at the weekend, however, both Rose and I liked to stay in bed a little bit longer, and I'd feed the horses later. But Siglen would worry away at his stable door until he managed to slip the bolt and escape; then he'd walk down the drive to our house and bang his hoof against the door until he woke us up. If we left the door open when he was around he'd simply walk in, just like a pet dog!

140

"Rose and I were here at the end, at the time when the Swanseas had to sell Caer Beris, and it was tremendously sad — but worst of all was losing the horses. Caer Beris was the biggest estate round here, with some seven farms and miles of river. But, of course, times were hard all over the country for the gentry. Death duties were beginning to break estates up. And Lord Swansea didn't manage the farms himself, or farm — he didn't really work at all. But soon the rents were not really enough by way of income, and he began to sell the farms to the tenants. It was a shock to everyone. Those last twelve months Lord Swansea tried everything to make some money — he even opened up Caer Beris to the public on Sundays; I used to sit at the gate taking the money, which was never enough, really no more than pocket money to them. Still, we tried, and we'd lay out all the silver, the porcelain, the trophies — everything was there to see. We even cut down some huge black firs lining the drive to try and make ends meet, but none of it made financial sense, and was nowhere near enough to keep an estate like Caer Beris going.

"It was terribly sad, but for us, the worst thing of all was taking the horses to Hereford market to be sold. Siglen went for 750 guineas, which was an absolute fortune in those days. Rose and I had already decided that if his buyers needed a groom then we'd go with him, wherever he went; we just loved him that much. I couldn't help remembering, during those sad days, how in better times I'd driven into Hereford for happier purposes — for instance, for the great house parties that we used to enjoy, the champagne would come from

London to Hereford Station, and I'd be sent in to collect it. There'd be loads of ice sent down as well, and we'd put it all in the old-fashioned type of hip-bath; then in would go the champagne, and that's how we'd serve it to the guests. Those are the times that I prefer to think of at Caer Beris, not seeing our favourite horse sold at auction. Yes, let's stick with the happy memories — like the time Rose made me a chauffeur's uniform when I had to drive the Swanseas down to see the Queen! That was another grand occasion for a young Welsh lad, I can tell you!"

"We were sad to leave Caer Beris," Rose added. "Very sad indeed. I look back on my time there with Jimmy as one of the happiest of our life. But you know, if we'd stayed on in service we would never have been able to afford a house like this in our older age. Jimmy was earning only £7 a week, which wasn't bad for that period, but never enough to actually afford a house of our own. And we were never done: we worked and we worked, and you never knew when you could put your feet up and say the day was done. I remember there used to be a wind-up phone in the stable house, and often it would ring at nine o'clock at night or even later, and Lord Swansea would be asking Jimmy to turn out to drive him down to Cardiff perhaps for the night train. When we had to have the room redecorated it meant taking the 'phone out, and we never had it replaced!

"It's nice that Caer Beris lives on, we both think. It's good that it's a hotel and that people can come from all over to enjoy it."

*

Epilogue

The hotel retains its atmosphere of grace. Hundreds and hundreds of houses like it have vanished, have decayed and been lost: today, the Smiths look after it beautifully. The panelled dining room is a joy; the sitting room is spacious and elegant, overlooking the grounds and the river; the bar — once the smoking room and Lord Swansea's office — is now snug and cosy. The grounds are still hauntingly beautiful, perhaps especially so in autumn when the copper beeches, which Jimmy planted some thirty-five years ago, are at their deepest, most fabulous colouring. The river, too, is still packed with grayling and brown trout, though nowhere near as many salmon run it as once they did.

"I love working in a hotel which has such history," says Catherine. "I wish I'd kept a book of people who come here, people who remember it, people who even worked here during the time of the Swanseas. I've been told so many stories of its past and I've forgotten most of them, sadly. The house has a lovely feel to it and I think the guests appreciate this. It's a site with history, you know, all rich and warm and tingly."

But Peter adds: "A place like this needs a tremendous lot of upkeep. It's a bit like the Forth Bridge — you can just never sit back and relax, there's always something needs doing. But it's worth it. Caer Beris is like a friend, difficult sometimes, but lovable through all. The people who come to stay, by and large, appreciate all this, and it means a lot to me and Catherine. We like to think that guests become friends . . . you could say that Caer Beris is almost a family house again."

Castle Howard

The building of Castle Howard, considered to be the third largest home in England, began in about 1700 and took nearly a century to be completed. Charles Howard, the third Earl of Carlisle, began the work and the family has lived in the house ever since. And what a creation Castle Howard is. Nobody has described it better than Horace Walpole writing in 1772: "Nobody had informed me that I should at one view see a palace, a town, a fortified city, temples on high places, woods worthy of being each a metropolis of the Druids, vales connected to the hills by other woods, the noblest lawn in the world fenced by half the horizon, and a mausoleum that would tempt one to be buried alive; in short I've seen gigantic places before, but never a sublime one."

Castle Howard is now owned and administered by a private company of which the Hons Nicholas and Simon Howard are the directors, both totally dedicated to the challenging task of running the estate and servicing the house both as a family home and as an important monument for the nation and the hundreds and thousands of visitors who flock to it annually. Both men remember, personally and with affection, Arthur and Ivy

Nelms, the Castle Howard cook and his wife, although it was really their father, George Howard, who brought them to the house and was their primary employer from the end of World War II.

When George Howard returned wounded from that war he vowed to move into the house that the family had left empty for over ten years; indeed, the family trust had already begun to sell off the contents, assuming that so vast a place would never be lived in again. Furthermore, fire had gutted much of the structure in the early 1940s and the thought of the Howards resuming their life there seemed impossible. George Howard, however, thought otherwise, and set about the task of restoration; he was helped in this by Lady Cecilia Fitzroy, daughter of the eighth Duke of Grafton and whom he married in 1949. It is this invigorating and exciting time that Arthur and Ivy remember so well.

Arthur Nelms, Cook Supreme

I travelled to see Arthur and Ivy in early June, although you would hardly know it from the atrocious weather conditions. The village of Welburn was simply awash, but inside their homely cottage, out of the rain and wind, everything was as snug as could be: a fire was crackling in the grate, and coffee, perfectly brewed, and home-made biscuits were instantly produced. We looked at their lovely garden through the streaming windows and then settled down to talk. Both Arthur and Ivy are in their early eighties, but you would certainly never know it: they are bright eyed and alert, and they obviously adore talking about their close relationship with the Howards and their great house.

We certainly weren't stuck for conversation. Ivy was continually bobbing off to fetch yet another gigantic photograph album, the print nearly always in black and white, nostalgic reminders of a world that we have all but lost. The memories, too, came thick, fast and vivid. "How is it," Arthur asked, "that I can remember absolutely precisely what happened to me fifty years ago, yet last week can be nothing but a blur?" Arthur was employed in 1947 by Christian Howard, George Howard's eldest sister. Arthur still has the letter of engagement offering him £5 a week, lodging free of rent or rates, two weeks' annual leave and two half-days free per week. There are no hours mentioned: Arthur was simply asked to complete all those duties expected of the Castle Howard cook — duties that he was to fulfil with total dedication for most of his adult life. The letter is a kind one: it begins "Dear Arthur", and this sets the tone, not just for the letter itself but for Arthur's entire life at Castle Howard. Christian Howard signed the letter personally, and one guesses that she actually typed it herself, too. All the Howards were obviously committed to the resurrection of the house, and making sure that the right staff were found to help in the great work was a part of the way forward.

Arthur is a lad from North Yorkshire who attended the grammar school in nearby Malton. Family misfortune stopped him setting off to find fame and fortune after school, and it was the war that took him away. He entered the army catering corps, and after hostilities ceased, naturally enough looked for a similar type of job close to home.

Ivy is also from Yorkshire, born in Scarborough which lies just twenty miles or so east, on the coast. She joined Arthur on the staff at Castle Howard very soon afterwards, first as a sewing maid hired to repair the household linens, but also to help in the kitchen when needed . . . which was frequently. The post-war Castle Howard was nowhere near the lavishly staffed palace of the past, and when Arthur arrived everyone helped out wherever and whenever there was a need. In fact when he first unpacked his bags, Arthur can remember being welcomed only by the family butler and by the ageing Nanny Stow, who had looked after George and Christian from one generation and was to look after Simon in the next.

"Oh yes, it was hard work all right in those days," said Arthur, looking nostalgically into the fire. "Neither Ivy nor I ever thought at all about the work, or about the hours. It just really wasn't in our nature to do so. The money wasn't an issue. We enjoyed our work, and we wanted to please and to do right by everybody. There was a real spirit of togetherness in those days, and both Ivy and I felt somehow to be more than employees. The Howards treated us as almost a part of the family, and that's how we liked to think of ourselves, as though we were all part of a team, making the house what it once had been."

The number of servants employed in the house has always varied over the centuries; often it would actually depend on how many children there were in the family at any particular time. Detailed accounts kept to the end of the nineteenth century by the ninth Countess recorded both the names of each of her servants and their position in the household. For example, in 1897 she employed over two dozen servants at Castle Howard alone, including housemaids, butlers, footmen, pages, nurses, charwomen, seamstresses, cooks and a pantry staff. Castle Howard was, therefore, a major source of employment in this remote part of Yorkshire, offering an alternative to a life on the farms, in the industrial towns or down the mines.

The lack of kitchen help certainly never bothered Arthur, and he had worked out an agreeable routine: "My Aga was fired with solid fuel and there were always several buckets of coke around the kitchen. I always had my old wireless on, too, and as often as not I'd be listening to the racing as I was preparing vegetables or making pudding. In my latter days at Castle Howard I was presented with a dish-washer, but I didn't really have a great deal of time for it, apart from putting glasses in after a big party or shooting lunch perhaps. I always reckoned that I could wash up quicker by hand, and sometimes I'd time myself just to make sure I was right. No, modern gadgets weren't really for me, although Mr George Howard was always coming in with something new, kindly thinking I'd appreciate it. The one thing that he did give me that really did well was a Kenwood mixer, which was useful for all sorts of things that I'd previously done by hand.

"Mr Howard travelled a lot by train, and whenever he was at a W. H. Smith's he'd look through the recipe section and bring me some book or magazine. By the end of my time at the hall I had a huge library stretching half the length of the kitchen!

"The kitchen was always a hub of activity, and there were always people popping in and out so I was never remotely bored or on my own. I remember Mr Howard's secretary coming in every day for cups of coffee to take back to the office; we'd natter for ages until a 'phone call would come through from Mr Howard himself, wondering what on earth was going on! I had Fanny and Johnny Craddock in the kitchen once, too, and got them to sign their books on the shelf! They'd been opening a village hall nearby and came back to the house for lunch. I'd served them their favourite, veal *cordon bleu*, which went down really well and they came to see me to get the recipe. What I didn't tell them was that it was pork fillet and not veal at all! In fact they were with me so long talking about cooking and what have you, that Lady Cecilia thought they were trying to fix up some deal with me to take me off into the outside world!

"The Howards were always fond of their food. In fact that goes back a long way into their history, because Isabella Byron, who was the mother of the fifth Earl Howard and some relation to the great poet, was a tremendous cook in her own right. She even wrote a book, which included such dishes as stewed carp and viper broth! I can't say that I ever came up with anything as exotic myself; but there were never any complaints. Mr Howard's favourite was always ice cream, home-made to my special recipe, and if for any reason I was absent, he would come out into the kitchen, sort out the ingredients and make it himself. When the family was away and things were just a little bit quieter, I'd prepare all sorts of sweet things for him: home-made jam, marmalade and bottled fruit all went down very well — and all the ingredients coming from the estate, of course. Later on, I'd freeze vegetables from the garden.

"We were very self-contained in those days; the milk, cream and poultry would all come from the farm, and we'd get all manner of game from the keeper, and make use of our own lambs. No, shopping expeditions were few and far between. I remember when that Canadian artist, Scott Medd, came over to repaint the Dome during the restoration — he needed egg whites for mixing his pastel shades, and he wanted dozens and dozens of them and they all came from the Home Farm. However, we even ran out of those, and I believe the gamekeepers chipped in with a few that should have hatched out into pheasants!

"Lady Cecilia tended to do all the menus for the week, and certainly for any special occasions; and Mr George was always one for special dishes — praline cake was one of his favorites. He had a very sweet tooth, he did, and he always wanted something a little bit out of the ordinary; I remember the young boys just pleading for something straightforward, straight roast beef for example.

"If Lady Cecilia was ever dining on her own then she'd almost invariably ask me to do a woodcock for her; she just adored them, she did. She'd eat everything and take them right down to the bare bones — she just loved to take her time and to pick and pick until there was nothing left. She'd tell me to knock off for the night and not bother waiting around, and said she'd clean up herself when she finished; but I know that was just to get me out of the way so she could have some peace for her favourite meal!

"Miss Christian Howard's birthday was in September, just as the partridges came into season, and so they were always *her* special dish. Birthday after birthday I used to prepare her a feast of partridges that had just been shot fresh on the estate."

Quite obviously, both Arthur and Ivy remember Mr George and Lady Cecilia with the greatest possible affection. To them — as to everyone connected with this great house — they were the instigators of the great revival, and yet were approachable with a sense of fun and always had a thought for others.

"Mr George used to get a bit irritated about all the talk in the papers over his eccentricities, but in fact all this came about simply because he liked wearing kaftans! He had been to India, I think, and had come across kaftans and enjoyed wearing them. It was as simple as that. He wasn't a hippie and hadn't gone wild or anything of the sort, he just liked the colour and the freedom of kaftans. The trouble was he couldn't get the sort of kaftans that he wanted, and so he used to come to me to make them up. 'Ivy,' he would say, 'make me something special, but don't forget the lining and the pockets!' He had to have pockets in his kaftans: if he went out and bought a kaftan it wouldn't have pockets, and then he'd have to carry all his stuff in a little bag over his shoulder, which he wasn't nearly so fond of. I think I made up something like half a dozen for him. I remember once picking up the lining for a kaftan from a jumble sale in one of the villages; it was a really nice piece of black material, and once it had been laundered and ironed it really did look the part. Mr George was very complimentary, but he never knew where I got it from, for that wouldn't have pleased him. He always liked the very best, did Mr George."

George Howard very much followed the traditional life of the family. Even during his high profile career at the BBC he used to take 'tastes' of Castle Howard with him, and Arthur would often be called upon to make the dishes to be eaten either on the train to London, in the capital itself, or even to be presented at board meetings! Without a doubt, Arthur's food fed thousands during his time at Castle Howard.

In the eighteenth century, John Atkins visited Castle Howard and wrote: "If our first parents, after being turned out of the Garden of Eden, had been immediately placed upon this spot of ground, they would have concluded that they had only exchanged one Paradise for another." It could be said that Arthur and Ivy felt the same way, that the bounds of Castle Howard provided almost everything they needed for a rich and satisfying life — almost, because their accommodation wasn't altogether perfect: for many years they lived in a flat just to the right of the Dome, in the body of the hall itself. Ivy remembers it as a lovely place to live, but terribly cold — in fact, once Lady Cecilia went to the top flat, just above theirs, and physically fainted after just a few minutes. There were pipes in the corridors but they weren't connected to the boiler until later on, and Ivy spent many a winter's night lying in bed swaddled in coats! One of the problems was that there were fifteen large windows all catching the elements, and as the flat was high off the ground, it used to be rattled by the wind. They had a kitchen, a sitting room, a bathroom and three bedrooms. Many times they were woken very early in the morning by peacocks that had got into the walled garden behind and were raiding the peas. Arthur would get up and throw oranges at them through the window until they flew back onto the wall and disappeared; then peace would reign once more.

Their flat had always been occupied by staff; before the Great War this had been the laundry maids. Household rules were very strict, and officially the girls weren't allowed out anywhere — but the local lads saw round the problem. According to legend — and Arthur actually remembers the stories — whenever there was a dance, the local boys would appear with ladders and the girls would descend, whirl the night away and then clamber back before dawn was breaking. If the Castle Howard girls appeared at any local dance it was immediately a sell-out!

Summer was particularly pleasant, and after tea, Arthur and his own children would often go to the north front where there'd be a cricket match going on with the Howard children. Arthur would play or coach until he was called away back to the kitchen to prepare supper.

Arthur and Ivy quite obviously felt very much a part of a big and happy family. If they had a day off, for example, Lady Cecilia would run them through the park to catch a bus or a train and then pick them up again on their return. Living at the hall was generally very safe and secure, a perfect environment for bringing up children. Once, however, back in the very early 1950s there was actually a break-in when a window was smashed and Mr George's office ransacked. The thief was caught very shortly afterwards and he confessed to another fifteen country house break-ins. It happened that his assault on Castle Howard coincided with one of the Nelms's days off, and when they got back the Howards all jokingly accused them of fleeing to spend the loot!

Castle Howard has always been a glamorous place in which to work, with the rich and the famous in almost constant transit. Queen Victoria, for example, visited the house in 1850: when Princess Mary called, however, George Howard was out at the York races; Lady Cecilia was at home and telephoned frantically around the racecourse until she made contact. George Howard rushed back whilst Arthur made the tea.

William Whitelaw came regularly to Castle Howard during Arthur's time, as did many people from the racing fraternity. One well-known gentleman amateur jockey called Heslop used to give Arthur tips — especially when he himself was riding a horse in the races. Arthur never lost a pound, and remembers the coming and going of guests as part of the exciting life he led at Castle Howard.

There were many diversions. Shooting parties and the annual farmers' dinner kept him busy . . . and all done on a skeleton staff. In fact these were days of relative modesty after the great parties that had taken place before the Great War, when thousands of poppies would be thrown over the balconies to welcome the guests to the house.

Castle Howard was often in the international limelight. Arthur has vivid memories of the filming of *Lady L*, directed by Peter Ustinov and which starred Sophia Loren and David Niven. Ivy particularly remembers Miss Loren as a demanding actress but one who appreciated things done properly. When she left at the end of filming she gave Arthur a signed photograph and confessed to him that she had actually developed a liking for Yorkshire pudding, although she had never tasted it before in her life. David Niven, however, was their real favourite: "Mr Niven was always popping into the kitchen," Arthur remembers. "He was great fun, always ready for a laugh and always picking at bits of food — in fact, when he left he signed a photograph for me saying, 'I'm going to sue you for making me fat!' The chauffeur would drive him from the house down to the pub here in Welburn, and Mr Niven would walk back on his own, often a good while after closing time!"

Best of all, in 1981 Granada Television filmed *Brideshead Revisited* at the house. Though it is not certain that Evelyn Waugh identified his Brideshead with Castle Howard, for many people these two buildings have come to epitomise nostalgia for pre-war England. In conjunction with Granada Television, the garden wall at the house was rebuilt, and Arthur has fond recollections of the filming itself: "Mr Jeremy Irons was an absolute gentleman. I'd always have to call him for any early morning shoots, and then he'd come into the kitchen for his breakfast, always washing up after himself. He was a very genuine man, I felt, as he used to sit there talking with us about the news of the day. There were times when his wife, Sinead Cusack, would come to visit him and bring his children and the dogs; actually the dogs could be something of a problem, and would occasionally stray into the set and whole scenes would have to be re-shot. I used to cook for Claire Bloom, too, who was a lovely lady and Sir Laurence Olivier would make appearances; he always wanted a pot of tea at exactly 4pm.

"I used to cook for any dinner party scenes. It used to be quite demanding because there would be lots of cuts and retakes and I would have to make sure that the food on the plate was always the same as it had been before the cameras were switched off. I think this is something called continuity."

Being connected with such a great house sometimes meant that Arthur and Ivy did more travelling than might be expected for a typical resident in this remote part of Yorkshire just after the war. When George Howard married Lady Cecilia in the spring of 1949 all the staff went to the wedding: they took buses to York station, from where a train sped them to London; there they were met and transported to St Margaret's at Westminster. After that they all went to the Hyde Park Hotel before having dinner on the train back home. The tenants and staff who were present still talk about this exciting outing to this day.

The year before this, George Howard had taken his cousin's house in Victoria through the season, the period when he was courting Lady Cecilia. Arthur was taken down to London to continue his cooking duties, but with many notable excitements. Ivy joined him from time to time, and they often went to the theatre — *Annie Get Your Gun* was a favourite. "Mr George and Lady Cecilia were very good to us indeed," Ivy remembers. "Lady Cecilia would buy us a box of chocolates to share when we went to the theatre, and she would make sure that there was enough money for a cab. But that was typical of the way that we were always treated. Even after the excitement of their romance, there would always be presents for me and Arthur under the tree at Christmas along with those for the rest of the family. That's how I always remember life at Castle Howard: I just felt I was a part of this very big and happy family."

Arthur confirms all this: "Mr George would often confide in me, especially later when he became ill. I remember, too, when Lady Cecilia became ill. She gave a cheque to me one day, a very handsome one, telling me that she had intended to leave it to me in her will, but had then decided that she'd like me to have it while she was still alive. She was ill for a long time, and often didn't know what she wanted to eat until twenty minutes before her mealtime; then I'd bend over backwards to prepare anything she might want.

"The night before she died, she sent for me and we talked for a long time. Even though she was close to death she remembered that I had a bad back and urged me to look after myself. She asked me to put her TV on for her, I left her and that was when she passed away. It was me that called the family together, and one by one they'd come sadly back to the kitchen where they would sit and talk and I would keep up, a supply of tea. That was a sad time, but then all families have these periods.

"Far happier — though it was sad for me and Ivy in many ways — was the retirement bash that the Howards gave to me. That really was a do, way back now, I suppose in 1980. Mr George was there, along with Miss Christian and all four of the sons. I remember that everybody met at 7.30 in the Great Hall, and this was followed by dinner at 8.15 in the Grecian Hall. We had printed menus, and I've still got one signed by all the Howards and the estate staff. We had melon Elizabeth, followed by turkey, and fresh strawberries that were flown in from Cornwall. The Castle Howard claret accompanied the meal, at which Ivy and I were both presented with engraved silver. I remember that all the Howards split up, each of them sitting at a different table; but that was typical of them. They tried to make everyone on the estate feel wanted, part of the life that went on there.

"Of course, retirement has been very nice both for Ivy and for me, and I know that we're lucky with this cottage in a pleasant village, close to the place that we've loved for so long. We keep busy and there's never a dull moment — but you know, talking about our life at the house and looking through all these photographs just makes me realise how rich our life was then, and how much we've both got to be grateful for."

Pitcastle

Pitcastle near Aberfeldy is a delightful Victorian mansion set in the midst of one of the most beautiful and peaceful areas of Scotland. The River Tay runs through the estate and Mr Kyd and his guests had regular successes in the salmon pools. From the river the land rises gently towards the moors. It is a rich, fertile area with profitable farming and excellent shooting. The moors offer grouse and occasional black cock, and the pheasant shooting can be exceptional. The varying topography which lies on the south-facing side of the valley is capable of supporting many wild birds: woodcock, snipe, chuck and pigeon. Brown trout in the moor lochs complete this sportsman's bag. Because of its setting in the sheltered Tay valley, this area is rich in history, dotted with ancient standing stones and earthworks speaking of a dramatic past. Pitcastle itself probably takes its name from the Pictish fort that once stood on the estate. On the high ground stands the "Clach-na-Buidseachd" or the Stone of Witchcraft, according to legend the site of many a coven meeting in times past.

As we move into the twenty-first century the whole idea of service might be considered a sad hangover from a less egalitarian past, when the class system was more entrenched, when secondary education was less universal, and when job opportunities — for women especially — were very much more limited. And you might be right, because in researching this book I heard, albeit at third hand, many unhappy tales of bad treatment, poor conditions and low pay concomitant with a life in service; the latter also frequently involved repetitious, menial and even downright unpleasant jobs, very long hours, appalling sleeping quarters and employers who treated their staff with the utmost disdain. However, all those whom I interviewed were positive and optimistic about their life in service, and look back with little or no regret. Rarely has this been more true than in the case of Mary Donald.

Mary Donald, Nanny and Family Friend

I met Mary on a stunning autumn day at her cottage in Strathtay in Perthshire. The November sun was streaming in through the south-facing windows, which gave a wondrous view over the valley of the River Tay. Everything was gold and brown, and the singing of the river in the distance made the setting truly magical. There had been a frost the previous night, but that morning Mary's small cottage — in fact a part of a bigger house called Dunros — was a haven of warmth and comfort.

"Oh, it's small all right," said Mary; "it has just one bedroom, a kitchen, a bathroom and this sitting room, but it does me splendidly. What on earth would I want with anything bigger, after all? I've never wanted to marry — no, I couldn't be doing with all that — and if my sister comes up to visit, it's quite big enough for the two of us. When Mr Kyd told me there was room for me here at Dunros, well, I was just pleased as Punch!"

Dunros is situated just beneath the imposing, whitewashed structure of Pitcastle, once occupied by the Kyd family, for whom Mary has worked nearly all her adult life. Mary Donald was born on 23 January 1918 on a farm at New Biggin, close to Dundee. Her mother had the thirteen children to look after — six sisters and seven brothers — and her father was a shepherd. "Oh yes, I came from a good home, and there's nothing in my life at all, certainly not in those early days, that I'd change. When I was just tiny I used to go and see the lambs with my father, and sometimes I'd help him take them to market in Dundee. We'd herd them along the road to the town with Roy, the sheepdog, worrying and snapping at them and keeping them in order. When I wasn't with him, sometimes my father would slip inside a pub for a drink or two, knowing that Roy would keep an eye on the sheep in the meanwhile.

"Once we'd sold the lambs we'd get the bus back to New Biggin, with Roy sitting there between us. It wasn't a big house that we had, by any means, but it was large enough for us. The boys were often away working anyway, generally on farms, and my sisters were soon off to work, most of them in service. But I've got to tell you that they didn't like it. They weren't as lucky as me, you see. Oh no, the Kyd family has always treated me special, like one of the family even.

"Life in service could be very hard indeed, and very poorly paid, too. In fact, that was just like my own first job where I was very badly treated. I couldn't bear the first lady that I worked for, and I was only in her house for two weeks before I walked out. I wasn't even fed properly, just on scraps from their table. I told my parents about it and they told me just to leave, which I did. It's never been like that with Mr and Mrs Kyd, let me tell you; I've always had exactly the food that's been on their table, and that's meant a lot to me. They've been good to me, all the family, and that's God's truth.

"When the war came I worked for two years in the foundry, but even though I was well paid, I hated it. Men and women worked together side by side in all the heat and the noise. It was the men's job to stack the bombs one on top of the other, and then we women would come along and stamp on the date. We called it the 'bomb shop', and I was forever getting my leg pulled by the men who used to say that I ought to eat more porridge to give me enough strength to lug the bombs around. I was glad when I finished there. It was soon after the war was over that I moved, and went to work for Mr and Mrs Kyd.

"As I remember, it was a friend who told me about the job; I cycled over to the Kyds' house and met them, and straightaway I was told the job was mine. The Kyds used to live in a big Georgian house at Broughty Ferry, about three miles from the centre of Dundee, sitting there on the Tay estuary; it was a wonderful place, and you could see as far as the Tay Bridge and taste the sea air. People were very friendly in those days, and I could take the children out in to the park to play with a wee ball perhaps, or just to walk, and I knew we'd all be quite safe.

"That was my job at first, to look after Gillian, David and Jane. I cycled in daily, I helped them get dressed, and then took them off to Miss Whyte's private school in Broughty Ferry. I'd see them again at lunchtime, then I'd pick them up in the evening and look after them until bedtime; I'd bath them and make sure they were settled down — and that was no easy job, let me tell you! I'd be sitting there underneath and hear pitter-patter, pitter-patter until I went up to sort things out. Mind you, they were very well-behaved little children. I'd creep up and say, 'What are you doing?!' and they'd hop back into bed at once. I never had any arguing back from them at all; they were very good, and always did what they were told. The great thing about them was that they weren't spoilt. Mind you, like all children they'd try and get away with things if they possibly could — for instance, you'd have to check over and over that they'd washed properly, especially their eyes, I seem to remember!

"It's important that children do what they're told. If ever the Kyd children were naughty they just wouldn't get their sweeties. They'd say, 'Ooh, Mary, ooh Mary!' but I'd simply reply, 'No, you've been naughty. Get up to bed right now!' I didn't smack them at all, I don't believe in that sort of thing, but they'd just know that they had to get up to bed and behave themselves.

"They had a good many friends, and very often these would come over to the house, for birthday parties and suchlike. Mind you, I didn't really encourage too much of this coming and going because, believe you me, there was a lot of work to be done with just the three of them! Still, you wanted them to have a good time; Jessie, our cook, was always there to make them a cake for special occasions, and as I've already said, I'd take them out into the park close by whenever we could, and we'd all play there; so they had an agreeable childhood, I think."

The family eventually left Dundee and moved to Pitcastle near Aberfeldy, some forty-five miles to the north-west. Mr Kyd continued with his legal practice in the city, but the family moved into the delightful Victorian mansion, which they began to renovate and improve. And Mary went with them: "I was never in any doubt at all that I'd move up to Pitcastle when the Kyds left Dundee. Mr Kyd told me that there was a home for me at Dunros, and I made up my mind on the spot. That's how it was, I was never in any doubt that I wanted to stay with the family. Of course, it's a bit more isolated up here, and Mr Kyd tried to get me to learn to drive; he even offered to buy me a car, but I truly think that all this driving and so on isn't really for the likes of me! But he was very kind, was Mr Kyd, and very often he would take me down to Dundee on a Friday morning, whilst he went to work, so that I could see my family. Then he'd pick me up in the evening and together we'd drive back to Pitcastle. But I've never felt cut off or lonely, because Mrs Kyd has always been very kind, too, and Mr Clark, the gardener, who lives at the gate to the estate, has always done me errands and taken me into Aberfeldy. So you see, I've never felt in the least isolated.

"As the children needed me less, I'd do more work in the house for Mrs Kyd, especially upstairs looking after the bedrooms. And then when Jessie got married and went to live in another house on the estate, I started to do the cooking. The family has never been one for heavy, elaborate meals — very often Mr Kyd would bring up a salmon from the river, and I'd cook that. He'd give me some pieces for myself, too; I love salmon. Of course, it wasn't quite like the old days when the children always used to eat in the kitchen with me and Jessie, and we'd have a lot of fun — but then again, I've always been looked after by the family.

"Even when Jane went away to London to work she didn't forget me. I went down on two occasions to visit her and each time she looked after me royally. The first time we went down together in an aeroplane — it was the first time I'd ever flown, and I think I expected something a bit more dramatic; in fact the landing was so smooth I stayed sitting there, and Jane had to tell me we'd actually stopped! She had a lovely flat, and she gave up all her time to show her old nanny the sights. I loved the theatre, and I remember we went to see *The Mousetrap* and *South Pacific*. We had lunch once at Fortnum's, which was something I thought an old lady like me would never do in all her days. Ooh . . . and then we went to Harrods' food hall — you've never seen anything like it — I just couldn't believe my eyes! We did all sorts of things: I loved going on bus trips, and we went to the very spot that the Fire of London started; we took a boat down to Kew, and once we went to the zoo. Everywhere we went, Jane took photographs of me, whether it was talking to policemen, standing outside the Houses of Parliament, or just being on the river. I've still got those photographs, and they remind me of some lovely times. I believe I developed a few sophisticated tastes down there . . . for instance I shall always hanker after the taste of smoked salmon!"

There is no doubt that the Kyds and their staff have formed a very firm alliance. One example of this loyalty can be seen in Mr Clark: when Mr Kyd died, the family moved out of Pitcastle and it was bought by the sugar giants Tate and Lyle. They wanted to retain Mr Clark, to look after the grounds — but there was no chance of this because he went with Mrs Kyd, to the bungalow she had had built lower down the grounds towards the river, to do the gardening and run errands for her. This fascinating man still fulfils these roles; he is also a piper with the Atholl Highlanders, the private army that many years ago was granted to the dukes of Atholl for ceremonial purposes by Queen Victoria. Mr Clark came into Mary's cottage whilst we were conducting our interview, with a bag of bread rolls sent up by Mrs Kyd — who, I must point out, is well into her eighties, too. He took a list of Mary's shopping requirements, and then departed, with a wave and a smile, into the sunshine. Shortly afterwards, Jane herself knocked on the door and came into the sitting room. And here is another happy story, because after leaving London, Jane returned to the Pitcastle estate and now also lives in Dunros, in the greater portion of the house, next door to Mary. David lives close by, too, although he is still working in the family's legal practice in Dundee. He is recently married and his wife has just had a young daughter — so there could well be nannying work for Mary once more in the near future!

"Oh yes, I feel very safe and well looked after here, and I consider myself lucky by any standards. For instance, I have a sister still living in Dundee, in sheltered housing, but although she's looked after nicely there, I know she's not as lucky as I've been. And I still have my uses — for example, until recently Jane had a cat called Dusty, a lovely creature, and whenever she went away I'd go in and feed it and look after it."

I'd finished my coffee and biscuits and the morning was drawing on; besides, Mary was giving me my marching orders: "Well, young man, thank you for coming calling on an old lady like me. But I can't be telling you anything else, because there's nothing else to tell. And mind what you write, because Jane will be asking me what questions you asked, and you'd better not go making anything up! If the book isn't right I'll be looking for you all over the place to give you a good kicking!" If Mary had said these words without that small smile on her face I would, I tell you, be seriously worried!

Hutton-in-the-Forest

Even on a cold, damp morning in December magic pervades the house that is Hutton-in-the-Forest. As you wander the grounds and the walled gardens the past seems at your shoulder, in no way remote, hardly lost at all. Perhaps this is because all is quiet. On a day like this there are no visitors. There is no jarring sound, just the call of birds from the extensive woodlands and the trickling of water from the streams. The wind plays in the trees, bringing the occasional whisper of sleet storms, but that is all.

Hutton-in-the-Forest is beautiful, not perhaps classically so with its jumble of architectural styles, but engaging, with huge character. It lies on the north-eastern edge of the Lake District, just over the hills from Penrith, and even today is surrounded by extensive woodlands, what remains of the medieval forest of Inglewood. Local legend links Hutton to the Green Knight's castle in the Arthurian tale of Sir Gawain and the Green Knight: perhaps this is the reason for its magic. The most impressive view of Hutton, and perhaps the most interesting historically, is from the front courtyard. From here the oldest remaining part of the house, the pele tower, can be seen tucked away in the far right-hand corner; originally it was moated. To the right of the tower lies the gallery, built in the 1630s, and on the far left is the huge neo-Gothic south-east tower. The centrepiece, the east front, built in the late seventeenth century is beautiful with its light-coloured stonework.

Raymond Morley, Stonemason

I'd come to Hutton to find Raymond Morley, a stonemason on the estate for forty-one years. I climbed the outside stone staircase to the estate office to inquire his whereabouts, and Lord Inglewood himself met me; his passionate enthusiasm and concern for the past, present and future of Hutton are the driving force behind the successful running of the estate. I was directed to a cottage on the fringes of the park where I was to find Ray at work on some restoration.

The walk to this cottage was once again through woods, with water everywhere, running in the ditches, singing away under a small bridge. Soon it was men who could be heard singing, talking and clattering, and I was about to find Raymond Morley; he was reslating the cottage, and came down off the scaffolding to greet me. "Yes, I suppose I'm a stonemason but there isn't a single job that I haven't done around the estate in the past forty years or so. If something needs doing, then I'm there to do it. Lord Inglewood says that we're all in it together, keeping the ship afloat, and I suppose he's right. It's his ship, mind, though — he's the captain!"

169

We went to the Upfront Gallery a few hundred yards down the road, a seventeenth-century barn that Raymond recalled before its conversion. "I remember they used to store grain there," he said, pointing past me to a stand of pictures and sculptures. "And cattle would have been housed through there." Today the old byre is a kitchen, with the most tempting of smells emanating from within. "It's good to see buildings used like this, not allowed to fall down and disappear. In fact nothing of the landscape around here has changed over the past fifty-odd years — not since I was a boy anyway, when I knew every tree and every stone for miles around.

"I was born two miles away from here, at a little village called Laithes; that was in 1941, and in those days we lived in a cottage belonging to a big house. It was owned by a colonel who was a farmer in a small sort of way, and had just moved to the area, from South Shields, I think. My mother was in service with the family and had come with them, and she eventually met my father who had been working on the Hutton estate. In fact, at that time he lived in the cottage where me and my wife are now! Pure coincidence, but interesting all the same.

"I went to school at Skelton, a tiny village, again about two miles away. The bus journey was one old penny — that is, if you hadn't spent the money on sweets! Walking didn't bother me at all. We were all used to it as there was little transport — nobody had cars, and buses were irregular.

"So you can see that our family is very much local. My grandfather even worked on the estate, not full time, but he did all the drainage jobs there. My father was a carter and used a horse all his days; his main job was to deliver the materials to the builders on the estate, generally slate and stone. Everything was done at a slower pace in those days. He would get the materials from the estate yard, the sawmill or the stone dump and take it here and there to whoever was doing what. Very little came in from outside, and they always used what they'd got around — beams, for example: old beams are well seasoned and don't twist and warp when put into a house. They kept all the old timber, stones and slate, so if a barn fell down everything would be saved. In fact it's still rather like that today, and everything is kept; you know, we even store toilets and cisterns and old baths! As long as they don't leak they're put to one side so they can be used later — you just never know when they might be needed.

"Childhood was a real one here for me. By that I mean that we never, ever stayed in the house, it was only for us to eat and sleep in. Nowadays kids never seem to go out, certainly not like we used to. But, of course, there was nothing in the house in those days; there was certainly no TV, and we only had radio at the weekends! Radios, for us, had those big chargeable batteries, a wet battery that you'd have to take to the garage to be all fired up; the women would walk to the garage each week with them, and you'd see holes in their coats where the battery fluid had leaked out! So we just roamed the woods and the fields, and we used our imagination when it came to keeping ourselves occupied. I suppose the world was a lot safer in those days.

"Everything was more simple. Our parents only really had three bills to think about: rent, fuel and food. Nowadays bills seem to come at you from everywhere, but it wasn't like that then. And living in the country there were lots of ways that you could cut down your overheads. My mother always baked her own bread and made our clothes, for instance. She'd make a cake perhaps with lapwing eggs that I'd found in the field. We ate a lot of rabbit — rabbit pie was always one of my favourites. And then Dad would go and see the local farmer when the potatoes were being harvested and ask if he could dig up the ones left in odd corners of the field. He'd take them to our garden, cover them up in soil and straw and we could store them the winter through.

"It wasn't all bliss, though — the toilet was fifty yards or so down the garden, and you'd have to take a kerosene lamp at night and put your wellingtons on if it was wet because the garden flooded. Your mind would wander, and you would imagine all sorts of horrors when you were sitting there at night with the lamp making shadows everywhere and the roof blowing in the wind!

"I told you that my mother worked in service, and her master, the colonel, was great with us lads. He used to have a trick, keeping eggs under his hat. He could sweep his hat off and there, neatly tucked away, would be four eggs. I tried it once and naturally enough broke the lot! I remember there was a big peach trellised up the house wall, and the colonel made sure that we had peaches the summer through.

"In the winter in those days you were used to being cold, and you'd sit huddled up in front of the fire while your back was freezing. We couldn't afford a chimney-sweep and used to clean the chimney just once a year. That was after Christmas when we'd push the Christmas tree up as far as we could and set light to it. All the soot would come tumbling down, and that would do us for the year.

"Even fuel we could save on. Mum and Dad would ask the colonel about a particular tree and get permission to cut it down. They'd go up with an axe and then use a two-handed saw to cut the trunk up. They'd then split the logs with metal wedges and carry the whole load back home. This would all be done by their own labour, and they'd store it up and we'd have wood enough to see us through the winter. You can't imagine women doing that sort of job today!

"I knew every inch of the landscape around here, literally every inch — I still think of it as my landscape, and I feel totally in tune with everything. I remember being told to keep out of a particular house, being warned that it was falling down; fifty years on and that house is still standing just as proud as it ever did. I recognise walnut trees from when I was a kid. Walking back from school — presuming I'd spent the bus fare — I'd cross through an area called Crow Wood. There was a big depression there, like a hole in the ground, and the colonel used to say this was the ever-open grave. The story goes that a butler at the house had got a maid into trouble. He'd dug the grave in preparation for her murder, but he'd got caught in the act and the girl was saved, and then nobody ever bothered to fill the grave in.

"I think that's how the word 'scrubber' emerged, because in those days girls that got into trouble like this were sent to other houses where they would do the most menial jobs, and that was nearly always scrubbing the floors. And they were often caught by their employers, you know, it wasn't just butlers and footmen by any means. Yes, they were hard times for lots of men and women in service. I was born at the start of the war, and really I've seen things get better and better every decade that I've lived.

"I came to work here on the estate almost immediately after leaving school — I often say that I came in with electricity! My first job was in the sawmill and I helped put the first electric motor in; it was second-hand, brought from the mines, but it worked perfectly. The foresters brought in the tree trunks for us and then we'd take over. We'd cut and shape all the timber that was used on the estate, and we'd make up whatever was needed. We worked with Scots pine, hemlock, Douglas fir and all manner of spruce. Then there were hardwoods — oak and sycamore for example, particularly good for lintels. The poorer timber we'd use for fence-posting, whereas the better stuff would be cut and air-dried for use inside houses. I used to make drainage boards out of sycamore and fit them to a lot of cottages on the estate. It was lovely wood, and you could shape the grooves in it beautifully. I even made a toilet seat or two in my time! That's the thing about working on an estate like this — you've got to be extremely resourceful! The old joiner's shop used to be a real museum. I remember there were cans of paint that they'd made themselves here on the estate, probably back in Victorian times. Unfortunately it was one thing we didn't actually use!

"Back in the 1950s when I first came to work here there was a lot more man-power around the estate: there were six men working in the forestry, and five in joinery and maintenance, so that was eleven, to start with. Today, there's nobody in forestry at all, and we're down to just two on the maintenance side. There's still just as much to maintain, but it's done differently, I suppose, and we do rely a lot more on outside contractors. The one good thing about being undermanned like this is that you have to do everything that comes along: there's no room for specialisation, and I never really know what each day is going to bring.

"At present I work with a joiner who does the electrical work, and we can be pulled here and there off any job. Not long ago, for example, the hot water system at the hall stopped working. What we found was a bat that had died and fallen into the water tank and blocked the pipe up! So detective work comes into it, too! Sometimes I'll be doing the decorating, or I might be hanging pictures or sorting out the drainage. Every year, Lord and Lady Inglewood put on plays here in the grounds, so very often I help the theatrical group get set up, running cables and setting up the stage — I'll be very much a part of the whole hustle and bustle of the event. Yes, you just never know . . . for instance, not long ago Lady Inglewood bought a colossal lead flower container which must have weighed between two and three tons. We had to manoeuvre this over the garden walls with a crane and then put it on rollers so that we could get it into its final position!

"Sometimes you'll even help out the chimney-sweep — one of the main chimneys in the hall has a crooked bit right up in the attic, and he can't get his rods round the bend. You have to climb up in the attic, remove some of the stonework, and then get in there with a shovel to actually physically remove all the soot. Then you have to put it into bags and carry it sixty steps or so down to the ground to dispose of it.

"A lot of the work involves maintaining the staff cottages. The house still has a cook and helper, and there is a chauffeur who doubles as a handyman and security person. Of course, this staff is very small compared with that of Edwardian times, and even when I first arrived there was a housekeeper, a chauffeur and three more who worked full time in the house.

"It's probably working on the fabric of the house itself, though, that I find the most interesting. You're always learning about old buildings, finding out something new, discovering how they did things in times gone by. For example, we've just finished converting a room, Lord Inglewood's father's office in fact, into a disabled toilet. This meant knocking through the pele tower, and I was daunted by the whole idea. The walls are six foot thick, you see, and totally solid, and I was terrified at the thought of what might happen — I was imagining the whole thing crumbling and falling down. In fact when we knocked the doorway through, not one single stone came down because everything on the outside is interlocked. So you have these interlocking stones on the shell, and the in-fill is all cobble and lime mortar — so you couldn't move a single stone unless it was forced. What I'm saying is that you come to understand how massively strong that pele tower was built; it really was planned to withstand a serious siege and bombardment. They made walls in those days like we can only guess at today.

"The fact that the house dates from all sorts of ages is interesting in itself. The important thing to remember is that only the best materials and workmanship went into the Hall during every era. With estate cottages, on the other hand, you'll find they would be built with the cheapest materials, with anything that was easily available. For example, one house I was working on was built with clay between the stones; this was to keep the stones apart and to make the whole building stable. But we had to put in a window frame, and as soon as we knocked through there was a trickle of clay dust and then the whole thing fell down! But the point is that clay was cheap, and the poorer houses had to make use of inexpensive materials. The Hall, however, is built of cut stone everywhere. An ordinary house would just have cut stone on the corners, and the rest would be filled in with cobbles and any old local commodities. It's like that all over the country — you might find Cotswold stone or Lake District slate here, there and everywhere. Where you come from, in East Anglia, it's the same too: houses would be thatched with reed and the walls would be made from the pebbles that they'd find on the beach.

"I still find the most satisfying part of the job is working with stone. I don't suppose I'm 'properly' qualified or anything like that, but I started at fifteen and a half years of age and I've been taught on the job — when I was just a lad I went with the old masons. One knew everything about drystone walling, and another was really good at brickwork, but neither of them could plaster, so I had to pick up that side of the business myself.

"I find working here truly rewarding. I try to put back into the work everything I can, and I'm always trying to hide the fact that I've been there at all, trying to make my work as inconspicuous as possible. You want everything you've had to do to blend in, to disappear, really.

"One of the great things about the job here is that you're never bored. You can wake up in the morning and think that you've something a bit tedious or depressing to do, you make a start — and then suddenly you'll be summoned to do something quite different altogether. I remember once I was working and I got a 'phone call to tell me that my own bedroom ceiling had fallen down! So I was away to patch that up.

"There are frequent surprises, too. For example, you often come across old coins when you are taking down ceilings. It's easy to imagine how they got there, too: a farmer or a forester or whoever would go upstairs to bed, take off his trousers, throw them over a chair, and loose coins would roll over the floor. They had no carpets in those days, so every now and again one would just fall down between the cracks in the hoards. It would lie there anything up to two hundred years or more waiting for me to find it. In this way you seem to develop a real sense of history. For instance, you can see where footsteps from the past have worn away the stone or the floorboards in the big house. And there are still scratches on the staircase dating back to the war when the army occupied it and the officers used to scrape the wood with their boots.

"I am lucky in that there is a great deal of job security here. The wages aren't particularly high, and there are no fancy pension schemes, but I do get my house and that counts for a lot. And I don't clock watch: if a job needs finishing, then I'm happy to stay on for half an hour or an hour to do it. It's that type of life here: you feel involved with both the family and the house; I believe we all feel ourselves to be a part of the estate in a real way. Lord Inglewood himself sets an example — he's totally committed to what we are doing, and thinks constantly about the house and the grounds. I know he only sees himself as a caretaker, looking after it for his son, just like his father did for him — but remember what I said about the idea of keeping the ship afloat? Well, that's how it is and it's good to work for someone who is so committed, so involved with it all, with so many ideas. He'll listen to what I say and understand what I'm trying to do.

"I've got another eight years to go before retirement, and I'll miss working here a great deal when I have to go. My mind is still as active as it ever was, but you know, your body does begin to slow down. I'm obviously hoping that we'll stay on in our present house, or somewhere else on the estate on a low rent. You never know what will happen in the future, but I would hate to leave the estate now, after all this while. If I won the lottery things might be different . . . but even then I don't think I'd like to leave the area where I was born and where I've lived all these years.

"Yes, I really have this sense of identity with the estate, and with the family as well, yes. I don't let this go to my head, of course, because inevitably there is a big divide between them and us. Yet here this gap is bridged a great deal, so that although you are on a different level, you do interact with them. Sometimes this can be tricky, and for instance you must always tread carefully between Lord and Lady Inglewood over sensitive issues to do with the house — in fact I'll often go to the agent and see what he thinks! You see, it's not like most jobs where your employer is remote or unknown; here, every task you undertake means a lot to your employers. It's rather like country schools as opposed to town ones: as a child at Skelton, every teacher knew the name and parents of every child in the school. Well, it's similar here, and we all know exactly what's going on. I suppose, to some extent, I feel that my life is controlled by the Inglewoods in that I work for them and I live on their estate — but you also gain a huge amount; for instance, I can walk in the gardens at night and smell the fresh air and just drink in the peace.

"And you are treated as part of the family, in a way. For example, I was invited to Lord Inglewood's twenty-first birthday party and his brother's eighteenth. I attended his parents' funerals, and actually helped to carry the coffins. I was at Lord and Lady Inglewood's wedding, and I joined in his brother's wedding party.

I've been to the christenings of all the three children.

"The wedding of Lord and Lady Inglewood took place at Keswick, at Fawe Park where Lady Inglewood lived — she's actually written a book on Beatrix Potter, did you know? Her house at Fawe Park was a model for Mr McGregor's garden in *Peter Rabbit* — and I'll never forget the sights of that wedding. There were tables on all the terraces with bottles and glasses, and drinks just everywhere! Then Lord and Lady Inglewood rowed across the lake and a cannon boomed, and there were fireworks. It was a remarkable spectacle. Mind you, it wasn't quite the sort of wedding that folks like us enjoy, because when you're a bit poorer a wedding for us is an excuse for a real banquet! As I remember there was oceans to drink, but only little bits and bobs to eat . . .

"I actually met Lady Inglewood years ago, long before she got married. I was up on a roof working when the late Lady Inglewood brought this young girl up, a student. She asked whether she could take my photograph, and of course I agreed. That girl is the present Lady Inglewood! She got to be quite a famous photographer and was friendly with Bailey and Lichfield and so on.

"There's some say the house has got ghosts — something to do with white ladies! People have said they've suddenly felt a wave of cold go over them, and that sort of thing; but I've worked on my own in the house a lot and never sensed anything at all. I've heard the place creaking and groaning, but it's just been the pipes, or the timbers or the stone settling. What I do believe is that somewhere in your brain you can generate your own visions, and I think some people can do this and others can't. It's all down to genetics, a gift if you like, something passed on within families. It's like Lord and Lady Inglewood's children: they're amazing, they're two steps up on the local children round here! I suppose to some extent it's having interaction with such gifted parents, but there's more to it than that — there are gifts and a special intelligence passed down from the parents. You see it in animals, too: how else do you explain how sheepdog puppies can round up sheep without ever having been taught it? These are just basic instincts, and I really believe we all have a lot of capabilities we don't realise we've got."

It was virtually dark when I left Raymond, the Christmas lights twinkling in his cottage. I drove up the hill and pulled in to take a last look at the big house settling into the twilight. A solitary electric light burned in an upstairs room, and but for that, it was a scene from centuries past. Soon, I was heading south on the M6, joining the queue for manic Birmingham, and thinking how fortunate Raymond Morely has been in his life spent at Hutton-in-the-Forest.

Trebah

It was exciting to be on the way back to Trebah, near Falmouth in Cornwall. I well remembered its famous ravine-riddled garden from a few years back when I attended a great party held there on a warm summer's evening. I believe the oysters we ate that night were fresh from the Helford river, so short a distance away that you could just hear the sound of lapping water from the verandah whenever there was a lull in the conversation.

The garden at Trebah is magnificent, planted in the 1830s and a century later deemed one of the most beautiful in England. At the start of the last war and after the death of its then owner, Mrs Hext, the estate was sold, and both house and garden fell into varying degrees of neglect until bought and restored by the Hibbert family in 1981.

That I sensed magic that night is, perhaps, not surprising, as Trebah is such an old and venerable place. For thousands of years the Helford river has been valuable for trade, and the Romans even farmed oysters there commercially. The place is first recorded in the Domesday survey of 1085, and for six centuries it passed by sale or marriage through many of the old Cornish families. The present house, quite lovely in its setting, was built in the eighteenth century by the Nicholls family.

The magnificent garden — open on a daily basis — really owes its existence to the energy and foresight of Charles Fox, whose family bought Trebah in 1826.

Charles Fox left Trebah to his son-in-law, Edmund Backhouse, in 1868; then in 1906, his son, Sir Jonathan Backhouse, sold it on to Charles Hext, a member of one of Cornwall's oldest families. Charles himself died in the 1920s, leaving his widow to continue the running of the house until her own death at the start of World War II. It is this later period that we will take a look at: Trebah through the eyes of F. Gordon Meneer, now an alert, charming gentleman in his eighties, but once a young footman serving at Trebah.

F. Gordon Meneer, Footman

"I was born at Wadebridge in north Cornwall on the 6 November 1919; I went to school in Bodmin. My very first job was at Trebah House, and I started when I was aged just fourteen. You know, I haven't had to think about what I am going to say to you in this interview at all — I haven't had to search my memory for any of the details because everything is still so fresh in my mind. I was only at Trebah for four years or so, but everything remains crystal clear, even how I got the job in the first place. You might well wonder that, because of course I lived about forty miles away at Bodmin, and generally people didn't travel at all in those days. Well, the rector of Bodmin used to come in to school every week, and he was a widely travelled man, with contacts in the higher circles of Cornish society. He knew Mrs Charles Hext down at Trebah, and had heard that she needed a youngster to learn the trade of footman. I don't know why I was picked — I suppose I was just the right age, just coming up to leaving school, and the rector thought I had the right sort of personality. Anyway, my parents decided that's what I should do, and so off I went.

"The rector, I remember it clearly, drove me down to Falmouth in his car and then I caught the bus on to Trebah itself. It was a day I'll never forget — you can imagine how apprehensive I was because I'd never been more than ten miles away from home in my entire life up until that moment. It was all a colossal adventure, and I was excited and nervous at the same time. I was fortunate, though, right from the beginning, because when I got there I learned that the butler, who was in charge of me all the time and teaching me the trade, was actually from Bodmin where his parents lived. This was great luck, and of course he accepted me then and there. It was really on that day that I reckon my education properly started.

"As I've said, I was a trainee footman and I answered to the butler. There were six indoor staff in my time: me, the butler, Mr George Sargent, the cook, the kitchen maid, the head housemaid and the under-housemaid. Yes, six of us just to look after this one widow! Mind you, the family had real money, and her husband had been High Sheriff of Cornwall back in the 1920s.

"My word, work was hard in those days, there's no doubt about that. The day began at 7.30am, and my first job was to wash, clean myself up and then get coal for all the rooms both upstairs and downstairs, and especially for the kitchen. I generally had to carry about six or seven coal buckets both morning and evening.

"Dead on eight o'clock we indoor staff would have breakfast in the servants' hall, all six of us together sitting at a long table. This would take us to about 8.30am, and then I'd go into the butler's pantry and make a start on cleaning up the silver and glassware from the previous night. The kitchen maid did all the pots, pans, crockery and all that sort of thing, leaving us with what were considered to be the valuable pieces.

"At 8.55am sharp, we would all assemble in the dining room. We sat on six chairs put there in a row, generally by me. Mrs Hext would come in and stand at the far end of the room and read a chapter of the Bible to us. Then we'd all kneel down for prayers. Can you believe it? What a way to start the day! How things have changed . . .

"Around 9.15am the prayers would be over, and we'd all depart to our different jobs. The butler and I got the breakfast from the kitchen, put it into dishes and took it into the dining room. Mrs Hext and any guests that she had with her then helped themselves, and we just stood by to make sure that the dishes were kept full. Breakfast was generally over at about ten o'clock, and the butler and I would clear the dining room and begin to wash the silver both from breakfast and the night before. By about 10.45am we were on to polishing it, and my word, every piece really had to shine. The silver cupboard was always clean — it was a point of honour that every piece had to really gleam.

"After that it would be my job to go round all the fireplaces in the house and lay the fires ready to be lit later on in the day when they would be needed. By now it would be getting on towards lunch time and the butler and I would go to lay the dining-room table. Mrs Hext very often had five or six friends to stay, and so there was nearly always the table to be set properly. The cook and the serving maid would pass food through a hatch in the kitchen into the butler's pantry, which was next door to the dining room. From there the butler and I would take it all in and serve it to the guests. This usually took about an hour or so, and we'd have our own meal after the gentry had gone — this was generally about two in the afternoon, back in the servants' hall.

"We've got to about mid-afternoon now, and my tasks then were to clear out the dining room and do any odd jobs that were needed. It always came down to me to go to the post office every single day to deliver letters from the house. I'd also collect any letters that had come in the second post and hadn't been delivered during the morning. I'd set off at about 3.30pm, and it would take me an hour or so to get there and back again. That was when I was walking! After a while I managed to save up enough money to buy myself a bicycle, and that cut down the time tremendously. Mind you, I had to buy the bike myself, I wasn't given it, even though it saved Mrs Hext quite a lot of my time. You've got no idea of the power of the bike! Of course, for the likes of us there was no chance whatsoever of a motor car, and a bicycle really opened up the world for you — in fact on some of the big estates it's hard to see how life would have functioned without the bicycle. Having a bike meant that you could carry messages and even carry hot food around; without one you were really a nobody.

"Anyway, around 4.30 in the afternoon it would be up to me and Mr Sargent to lay the table in the dining room again, this time for tea. We'd put out the cups and saucers, the cakes and the sandwiches, and the guests would help themselves, much like they did during breakfast time. We'd have our own tea after that, generally about 5.30pm. At six, the butler and I would clear up from afternoon tea and then have an hour or so off. Mind you, there wasn't a great deal you could do with that! There we were, stuck out at Trebah, miles from anywhere, so at best all you might do was read for a bit or have a short nap.

"At seven we were on again, this time laying the table for dinner! Yes, four big meals every day, that was how the gentry lived in those days. Dinner was the highlight of the day, certainly for Madam. It was a real ritual, and generally a four- or even a five-course meal. We had to set out dessert plates with doilies on them in front of every guest, and then a little finger bowl so that they could wash after peeling oranges, pears or any sticky fruit. We also had to lay three glasses by every place — a tumbler for water, a claret glass, and then a straight wineglass so that the guests could have exactly what they chose. At first the wine was served by Mr Sargent, but little by little I began to understand things a bit more and sometimes I would do the job.

"At 7.45pm it was my job to bang the gong to summon Mrs Hext and her guests to dinner. They'd all take their places and say prayers — they did this before all meals, but in the evening it was an extended operation, a very long grace indeed. How long the dinner lasted rather depended on the number of guests. Five or six people was about average, and they'd finish around 9.30 or so in the evening. Mr Sargent and I would then begin the job of tidying up and making ourselves a cup of tea . . . it would be late then, and there was very little else for us to do than get off to our beds.

"That is how a footman generally spent his day — and it was a long one, believe me. But it was a long day for everybody then, and especially when you worked in the kitchens. The kitchen maid, for example, was responsible for keeping the range alight, and this would mean that she'd have to get up before everybody else to rake out the ash and get it going so there'd be hot water. The housemaids were responsible for everything that went on upstairs, looking after the beds and keeping everything spotless. They'd also look after any guests, and they wouldn't be allowed to go to their beds until they were quite sure they wouldn't be needed for anything.

"You had to be adaptable, of course, and do any job that might come up. Take the summertime, for example, when the guests wanted to go out in the Trebah boat — yes, in those days we had a full-time boatman, as well as a chauffeur and six permanent gardeners! You can see the sort of money that it took to run an estate to the highest standards. Anyway, on a nice day the guests

189

would often decide that they wanted to go out sailing in the estuary. The boatman would bring the yacht round, anchor it offshore and then come into the beach in a smaller dinghy with an outboard motor. It would be my job to bring the huge picnic hamper down from the house to the beach where it could be loaded up. I had a wheelbarrow especially for the job. Naturally it had to be clean, absolutely spotless, so nobody else was allowed to use it for any other job whatsoever. It was all right pushing the hamper down because of the lie of the land, but bringing it back up was quite another job, I can tell you!

"Apart from that hour or so between six and seven in the evening we'd be pretty well expected to work a fifteen- or sixteen-hour day. We did get half a day off every week — on a Tuesday afternoon — and Sunday afternoon once a fortnight, and that was considered quite generous. We also had a two- or even a three-week annual holiday, which was paid as well. Mrs Hext loved Portofino, in Italy; she would often go there for a month at a time, and when she was gone, that was when we'd have to have our own holiday. Some of us would stay to look after the house, and so we took it in turns. Every year this was my chance to get back to Wadebridge, and I'd generally ride all the way, over forty miles, on my bike. I used to look forward to the journey itself because there was hardly any traffic, hardly any cars anyway, and most of the dust would be kicked up by horse traffic. Mr Sargent had a motor bike and if our holidays coincided and if he decided to go back to Bodmin, then he'd take me with him, sitting on the back. Yes, he was good to me, was Mr Sargent: he was only a small man, I remember, but he really knew his job. He had a bad bit of luck in the war because his parents were killed by bombs — yes, in Bodmin! I think only three bombs ever hit the town, and one of those landed on his house.

"I remember when I arrived at Trebah I was *told* what the pay would be — I certainly wasn't asked, and there wasn't the slightest chance of bargaining! Yes, I was told my pay would be £18 each year. The drill at every country house was that you were paid in twelve monthly instalments — so in my case, of £1 10s [£1.50] each! The money was paid in cash on the first day of the following month. Of course, £18 was never a fortune, not even in those days, but I did get my food and a new livery every twelve months. I wore a charcoal grey suit with a white shirt and a black tie — at least, certainly from lunch-time onwards when I was expected to look the part. Of course, I paid no rent or rates or anything like that at all, and even my washing was all done for me. Just off the estate there was a small hamlet with six cottages and a laundry; one of the gardeners lived in the laundry house, and his wife did all the washing for the whole house. This was a pretty big job because there was all the clothing for the staff, Mrs Hext and any guest, as well as all the towels, sheets and everything else. Mr Sargent also had a starched collar to go with his bow tie, and that was all done for him as well. So you can see I didn't really have many responsibilities apart from doing my job well.

"I used to try to save some money, but I never really got very far with that. Every Tuesday afternoon I would go straight into Falmouth. I'd have something to eat there, and then I'd be off to the pictures. The under-housemaid was also off on Tuesdays, and sometimes we used to go in together on the bus. I think I can tell you now that we used to be very fond of each other, if you know what I mean. Not that anything came of it at all. Oh, no — Mrs Hext would never have allowed that sort of thing!

"Mr Sargent and I shared one room, with a couple of single beds in it, and we had a bathroom to ourselves; this was on the first floor, in a different wing to the one used by Mrs Hext and the visitors. The rest of the staff slept on the third floor. I've got to say that we all had nice rooms, and they were cleaned and looked after by the housemaids who also laid out clean clothes for us. Our food was top quality, too — we had just about the same as what went to the main dining room. We were very lucky indeed in that way, because not all staff were treated as well as this, let me tell you. Yes, if they had beef, then so would we. So you can see that for a working-class boy like me I really lived a very upper-class style of life: there I was in a grand house, with a very pleasant room, totally looked after, and enjoying some of the best food you'd ever eat. Obviously there were drawbacks to the job, but my days at Trebah gave me a taste of a lifestyle that I would never have been able to afford for myself.

"Mrs Hext had great power over us, pretty much total control. She even made the under-housemaid change her name, would you believe, because she didn't like her real one! But — and this is the big thing — we were always treated well. I can never remember any dispute at all. Everything was good and above board, and she'd think about us a great deal. For example, whenever she came back from Italy she'd always bring a present for all of us who worked indoors. It might be clothing, or an ornament, or some item for our respective bedrooms, but whatever it was you knew that it would always be something of quality, never anything cheap, and chosen with care. It was an aspect of Mrs Hext that we all appreciated.

"In those days she was a Justice of the Peace, and used to sit on the Bench up in Bodmin. Whenever she went up there she would take either Mr Sargent or me with her because she knew that we came from the town. She had two cars, and we'd generally go in the larger one, an Austin Twenty I think it was. On my first journey I sat in the back, obviously dressed in my official livery. The hood was down and I had nothing on my head so my hair blew around a bit. The chauffeur dropped Mrs Hext off at the courtroom and then took me home. As we were driving along he told me that I had to get a cap; he said that whenever I was out driving with Madam it was impolite to go bareheaded. Can you believe it? Anyway, that's the way things were, and I told my parents. So my father went out and got me a cloth cap just for those few journeys up to Bodmin with Mrs Hext. That's typical of the distinctions between the gentry and the rest of us — today's workers just wouldn't accept it at all I don't suppose, not for a moment!

"The guests at Trebah were nearly always either relatives or close friends. One of Mrs Hext's relatives was an MP for Falmouth and he used to bring with him a lot of cronies from parliament. The guests tended to be the same people, so we'd get to know them pretty well. They were invariably nice, as I remember, and they got to know us over the years, especially those that came four or even five times a year. Things were a lot more leisured in those days, and they'd stay quite a long time. The butler was always addressed as Sargent, but me, I was always known by my Christian name, Gordon; I suppose that's because I was just a boy and not in any particular position of authority. I was very impressed with all the guests at first because they were rich and well mannered and they always dressed up for dinner in tails with white tie and so on.

"When they were leaving, we would always see them out to their car, or if they hadn't come in their own, to one of Mrs Hext's. We'd carry their luggage for them and wish them a good journey. They always had a tip for the butler and for me — but they'd never give anything to the housemaids or the kitchen staff! That was a bone of contention at Trebah, and in every other house I knew about. The butler was given about 5s [25p], and I was generally gifted 2s 6d or perhaps 3s [12$\frac{1}{2}$p or 15p] if I was very lucky, never more.

"Mrs Hext used to get cross about tipping and would tell them not to do it. I'm not quite sure why she was offended, but we took great care to hide the fact that we got the money. Three shillings . . . my God . . . I used to think I was made! You see, the pictures only cost nine old pence or a shilling, so a good tip meant I could go for free for three weeks!

"Talking about guests brings me to Easter Sunday, 1935. Well, at ten in the forenoon I was sent to the village with a letter to deliver to a couple who were supposed to be having tea at Trebah. Mrs Hext just said that their visit had to be cancelled and didn't immediately give me any reason why. It was all a bit mysterious, but I soon found out the reason: in the mid-afternoon a car arrived, and out got the Prince of Wales with his friend, Mrs Simpson! There was also Mrs Simpson's husband and another couple of friends. Oh yes, it was a very secretive job indeed, one which was kept very, very quiet — *nobody* in the village knew anything about it at all, and I don't really think they believed us for a while afterwards.

"We prepared tea, nothing special, just what would have been laid out ordinarily — it was just like any other at the house. But let me tell you, they were a charming party. Mrs Simpson obviously had her detractors, there's no doubt about that, but I could tell at once she was high class; it really stood out — she might not have been royalty, but she really *was* high class. The whole occasion went perfectly. After tea, they just got up and left quietly with no ceremony and no fuss. It was a great, great honour and I'm always glad that I had the chance to serve people like that. Mrs Hext was not in royal circles, of course, but she was a member of the local gentry and that's how it came about, I guess.

"After tea had been taken I remember the Prince of Wales sat in the garden smoking a cigarette. These were specially made for him, and he only smoked half of this particular one. He stubbed it out in a flowerbed and we found it afterwards and kept it in a cupboard for six months! We even marked the chair that he'd sat in so that we could tell people in the future. After the scandal, Mrs Hext was furious. She just couldn't take it at all. All memory of the day was swept away and no mention of it was ever made again. However, before they left they all signed the visitors' book. This was lost after Mrs Hext's death and when the estate was sold, but it came up recently again for auction. Major Hibbert was out of the country at the time and couldn't make the auction, but his wife bought it for about £400, so now it's back where it belongs. A nice story I think, that.

"They were great days really, and for me those four years were a real education in themselves. I just learned so much, things I would never have guessed at if I'd stayed at home. All us indoor staff were close. We all got on, we just had to, being in such a small community. We'd sit in the servants' hall, having our meals, gossiping about our families, our work and all sorts of topical stuff. Sometimes, though, we were just so tired we didn't say a thing! I suppose we were all working class, but we all realised that nobody lived better than we did. We all felt just a bit privileged. I certainly don't regret a single day I spent at Trebah.

"I left in 1938, though I was reluctant to do so. You see, I'd fallen properly in love with a girl in the village, a farmer's daughter. We were so fond of each other that we just couldn't bear meeting up on only one afternoon a week. I didn't want to leave, but that was it. If I was going to have anything like a normal relationship I had to. I took to gardening, which meant that I could meet my fiancée every evening. I began to work as a gardener and then joined the Navy in 1940. We got married in 1942, and we had our son in 1944 — but that's another story! After the war I didn't go back into service but carried on with my gardening until I retired a couple of years ago.

"I was sad when I heard that Mrs Hext had died in 1940. She'd been good to me, and I felt had helped make me the man that I'd become. The estate was sold and resold four or five times before the present owners took over. Of course, they've had to commercialise it, and even though they've done the job very well, very tastefully, Mrs Hext will no doubt be turning in her grave every time a visitor goes through the gates! She was conservative through and through, and I don't think she would have ever foreseen a time when the general public would have been walking around her beloved gardens. But that's how things have changed. I reckon that I'm lucky to have lived through those days at all."

Tulchan Lodge

Tulchan Lodge close to the River Spey, is a large, imposing stone building that was completed in 1906 to the order of George McCorquodale, the proprietor and chairman of the printing and publishing group of that name. When first built, the house was known as Dalchroy House and, as a Scot and holder of a tenancy from a Scottish peer, Mr McCorquodale was able to style himself as G. F. McCorquodale of Dalchroy. He originally came to know the estate as a guest of the banker Sir Philip Sasson, a close friend and financial adviser to Edward VII. Sir Philip was the shooting and fishing tenant at the original Tulchan Lodge, situated some two miles to the west of the present house. So enamoured of the area did G.F. become that the new, large building was constructed. Tulchan estate was a sportsman's paradise, especially in the period between the wars. G.F. was a very persistent, skilled and effective fisherman and he fished the estate waters for four months each year. The total number of salmon caught by him on the Tulchan estate was 4,836 by the time he died in 1938.

After G.F.'s death the McCorquodale tenancy at Dalchroy and all sporting rights automatically reverted to the Seafield estates as there was no surviving male heir. On taking possession of Dalchroy, the Earl of Seafield renamed the house Tulchan Lodge, as it is known to this day.

During both the World Wars, the houses and cottages adjacent to the lodge were used as a convalescent hospital for servicemen recovering from their wounds and apart from some local use, no formal fishing or shooting took place. The grouse moor had always been an important aspect of Dalchroy life, indeed the estate's moors were known as some of the best in the United Kingdom and among the royal guests who shot on them were Edward VII, George V and King George VI as Duke of York.

Dalchroy House was a very special place and so it remains today in its new role as an international-class hotel. The standards of comfort and service provided in the now-named Tulchan Lodge are of the highest and the guests are still attended by a butler, under-butler, housekeeper and a very full household. Indeed, even today, it is possible to appreciate how it must have looked and felt in its heyday when a young Janet Irvine worked there.

Janet Irvine: Memories of a Life in Service

It was when Dalchroy House was in its prime that the delightful Mrs Janet Irvine was employed there. She worked in many great houses during her life in service, but centrepiece of her career were the years between 1928 and 1934 when she worked as a kitchen maid at Dalchroy.

I met Janet Irvine in the strangest of ways. I have friends at the Freshwater Fish Laboratory in Pitlochry, Perthshire, and on one of my visits noticed that all were wearing extraordinarily fine socks underneath their thigh boots. When quizzed about these they told me they were knitted by a remarkable elderly lady presently resident in Nairn, Inverness-shire. When I also learned that she had spent a lifetime in service and had some fascinating recollections, I decided to pay her a visit.

Janet Irvine could not have been more welcoming. When I arrived she was already waiting for me in the lobby of her residential home: alert and attractive, I was proud to have her as my companion in the hotel restaurant that day. She rewarded me with a whole host of memories, every detail pin-sharp.

"I was born Janet Martin on 31 October 1914, at Halloween on the east coast of Scotland. My dad was an estate worker with the then Earl of Leven. I started school in 1918 when my dad was fighting in India. I was just four years old, and me and my sisters had to walk nearly three miles and stay in school until four o'clock. In 1920 there was a heavy snowfall, when I was just six and my sister Annie ten; the snow was up to our knees, but even so, we were strapped for being late. I can still see my dad striding into the classroom the next day, furious with the teacher for strapping us. But that's how things were in those days. Life could be very hard.

"The house we lived in then was manse property, owned by the church. As well as being the gravedigger, my father had to be beadle, that is being an officer in the parish and keeping order in and around the church. It was an important role in those days and required father to inform everyone of meetings and any church business. One day a man called with a white box under his arm. I mistook it for the white box full of chocolates that the Lady Leven often carried with her in her chauffeur-driven car; it was all engraved in gold, and she'd open it up and give us a chocolate. But this white box carried the little body of a stillborn baby. I can remember it as clearly as yesterday.

"The teachers that we had were quite fair to us, on the whole. My first headmaster at Hopeman School was a Mr Hunter, who'd been a Grenadier Guards officer in the 1914 war. This was my secondary school, and there were forty-six pupils in my class — it is so sad to think that many of the boys I was at school with lost their lives in the last war. We had a janitor then, too, a Mr Fletcher, who was also called the whipper-in. If a child was absent from school it was his job to go to that child's home to find out why. Nearly all the boys in my class became skippers or seamen of one sort or another. They were born within sight and sound of the waves, and the sea was in their blood right enough. I remember one boy, John Sutherland, in particular. He was a big lad and was hardly ever in school 'cause all he wanted to do was to get to sea as soon as he could. Sealing and fishing was bred in him, but one young lady teacher had the right idea: she struck a deal with John, that he would come into school from Monday to Friday, and in return her brother would take him out in his boat over the weekend. It worked, and John Sutherland was a good pupil until he left to go to sea full time.

"All the boys were given navigation lessons at school from the age of twelve. The classes were well attended, and many of the boys then went out to sea with the line fishermen who taught them to navigate by the stars. One story goes that during World War II an ocean liner called the *Arundel Castle* was torpedoed, and one of the young lads from Hopeman School found himself in a lifeboat full of brass hats. They all laughed at his idea of steerage by the stars — all the compasses and so on had been lost — but the commander spoke up for him, and under his guidance they all reached land and were saved.

"When I was a little girl, Hopeman harbour was full of steam drifters going to fishings at Grimsby, Lowestoft and Yarmouth; they would come back with furniture, crates of dishes, even garden tools and wheelbarrows — all the things we needed for the households up here. Many of the men were line fishermen, older men who fished with long lines baited with mussels. Each day their lines were baited by their wives, who would walk the five miles to Findhorn to get the mussels; their shawls would be wrapped in a piece of oilskin as protection against the salt water and they would wear stout serge skirts and long laced boots, and they would all have bandages on their fingers because the knives for shelling the mussels were so sharp. They were a tough breed, all of them, and hardly ever ill. A newly set basket for fishing was a lovely sight, with all the bait laid out like soldiers.

"Hopeman was a tight, caring community, and certainly before the last war the people would all help each other out. For instance, if a mother was going to

202

Elgin by bus she would simply put her kiddies into the house next door and she knew they would be safe. Nowadays this would probably be called child neglect, but at that time everyone did it — everyone helped each other. I think you will find there are no kinder people anywhere than fisherfolk, especially the older ones. Aye, I've seen changes, and not always for the best.

"When we were children we'd walk along the harbour side and often the older men would give us a fry to take back home, maybe a dozen smallish haddock that were too small to be sold at the fish markets on the quayside. Everything was about fishing. At the time it was common to see old fishing boats turned upside down by people's houses, and these would act as coal sheds. Remember this was in the 1920s before any council houses were built, and all houses were either owned or rented. The local policeman kept law and order all on his own — even the sight of his uniform was enough to keep order! I don't think there was much stealing then, and in fact all round the coastal towns very few people even locked their doors.

"My mother belonged to Hopeman, and her people were all boat builders or line fishermen. Her uncles all served in the 1914 war on minesweepers, and I used to hear them tell of their experiences and the rescues they carried out after boats were torpedoed. The war preyed on every man's mind in those days in the 1920s. I had one headmaster, a Colonel Reed, a true army gentleman who used to teach us geography. But I can tell you, it didn't matter where we were talking about, he'd always come back to Vimy Ridge.

"We did religious studies at school, and it is interesting that fisherfolk all around the coast were very religious — I think one reason for this is that their calling was so hazardous. The fishermen in drifters had a particularly hard life, and didn't have any modern medicines; if they fell ill, then they would just have castor oil or some good toddy — surely it was kill or cure for them. Unemployment was not a problem at this time because everybody kept themselves very busy indeed; thus fishermen who were too old to go to sea mended nets — they laid them over a bar of wood between two uprights, like goalposts — or they'd cure their own fish in sheds separate to their houses. And keeping myself occupied was to be the pattern of my own life, too. I left school at fourteen, even though I was clever at it, and went straight off into service with the McCorquodales. This house, Dalchroy, was owned by G.F. McCorquodale, a millionaire. His firm were printers and publishers, with business in Glasgow, Liverpool and London; their headquarters were in London.

"When I was in school I sat next to the Dux, the best pupil in the school. This was an honour and it showed just how well I was doing but schooling made no difference in those days if you were a girl in a family of eight — and I was one of eight — well, you just had to get out and work. I was barely fourteen when I became scullery maid, and I had all the dishes to wash from the dining room. This was worse than having the ones from the pantry, because in the pantry there were just four men, a hall boy, a butler and two footmen. You did whatever you were told — and that housekeeper could shout at you, I assure you! And we had copper pans to clean because the dining-room food was made in copper pans. Everything had to be chopped, and if the fruit was for a mousse or any kind of compote, it all had to go through a sieve. The McCorquodales wouldn't eat tinned fruit unless it was brought to boiling point and the syrup thickened and possibly with cochineal put in; the lady of the house was dubious of anything in tins.

"I was two years as scullery maid, and then I was second kitchen maid. That meant you had to boil up all the gravies and the soups, and get stockpots going; we had to fillet fish, and pluck hens, grouse and pheasants, anything that happened to be brought in. We also had to skin rabbits and hares, and when you skinned hares you kept the blood for hare soup.

"We never saw the boss, only the housekeeper: if you wanted to give in your notice you told the housekeeper, and if you wanted a rise you told her — and inevitably she would say, 'Oh well, the lady's not prepared to give it to you until you're twenty-one'. I got only ten bob a week for all those years — over in that kitchen from six in the morning until half past eleven at night: I was never out of it. We'd to bake in the afternoon, everything was hand-baked. We had to make bread and buns and cookies, and all the cakes for the dining room and for the servants' hall. We'd to wash all the dishes in the kitchen at night, and at very last thing I had to wash in front of that stove. It was pure slavery!

"The late twenties and early thirties we called the Hungry Thirties; there were huge numbers on the dole, and the housekeeper used to say to any of us, 'You know, if you're not pleased there's plenty of others waiting to take your place'. But when I left, the ones that did come were girls that had worked in factories, and of course they said, 'We're nay plucking chickens and filleting fish', and they wouldn't do it. But if, for any reason, you got the sack at that time, well, you had difficulty getting another job.

"We had another bonny scullery maid called Lillian, for all the world like Marilyn Monroe, and the butler, he used to come on after Lillian. But I felt responsible for her, and I used to just bulldoze him out of the kitchen; I'd say, 'You're not coming in here while I'm here!' because I knew too much of the world to let him in. This little girlie Lillian, she was only sixteen and vulnerable, and I felt I had to protect her.

"At one of the houses I worked in there were seven footmen. One chap that worked in the kitchen — we called him Ginger, but Albert was his real name — he'd worked for the Prince of Wales before he married Mrs Simpson. Apparently at Fort Belvedere, if Mrs Simpson and the prince were going to see any of the latest films, she would allow the staff to go in and sit at the back, providing they were quiet. Everyone thought the world of Mrs Simpson. When they married, quite a lot of the prince's staff came to work for the Duke and Duchess of Windsor, and they praised her to high heaven, saying how kind she was, and what a beautiful person. What the papers had to say about them at that time was terrible, of course, and we had a dreadful time, too — we would prepare dinner, and then nobody would come; it was very, very difficult.

"I respected all the people that I worked for, they were all extremely kind; if you met them outside they always spoke to you. At the Duke of Windsor's you always tried to look clean and 'jacoos', as we say — that is, as perfect as possible. I remember there was one housemaid at the Duke of Windsor's who always looked as if she had slept in her clothes. I mind one time, we were in the servants' hall and Albert turned her round and he said to her, 'Look, you're not going out of this establishment looking like that! Take off that skirt and I'll press it'. And do you know, she had her coat on ready to go, but she whipped off her skirt as if it were just tomorrow, and a whole lot o' women in — and she never jowed a' ginger!" It obviously amused Janet hugely that I had to ask what this meant, namely to blush, or not to be embarrassed. And equally obviously, any maid who in that day and age took her skirt off in the presence of a butler — albeit from underneath a vast winter coat — should indeed have jowed her ginger to the utmost!

"Between the 1914 war and the time that I went to work in McCorquodales there were about three million domestic servants; but as time passed the gentry were too heavily taxed to be able to keep a lot of servants — it was too much, and now, of course, they have to depend on home helps."

Lunch finished, Janet and I went into the dignified drawing room where she settled herself on a colossal settee with impressive drapes behind her, looking more the mistress than the maid. Over a cup of tea she told me more of her life in service at Dalchroy.

"Mr G.F. McCorquodale, the owner — we always called him just G.F. — built a huge extension to his garage in the 1920s, after the Great War, which initially was used as a convalescent home for officers and ranks. Here they could fish and walk and generally recuperate, and over the next few years a great many lived there and did themselves great good. All the officers ate in the dining room, whereas the ranks took their food in the kitchen.

"Later, when I was first working there, this extension became the servants' quarters — all the visiting toffs had chauffeur-driven cars, the ladies had maids and the gents valets, and if any guests brought horses with them, then there would be grooms, too. It certainly accommodated the chauffeurs and valets once the soldiers had moved away, though the extra maids would be put up in the house itself. This made the house very busy, because there were four servants to each department — four in the kitchen, four housemaids, four in the pantry as well as my lady's own maid and G.F.'s secretary. When the house was really busy like this, G.F. would ask his chauffeurs' wives to come in to help out. G.F. kept three chauffeurs, three gardeners, a joiner, a handyman and about ten ghillies and a great many gamekeepers, so you can see what a huge estate it was!

"G.F. had one gamekeeper — or 'gamie' as we always called them in those days — who reared Labrador retrievers. He sold them all ready trained, and even in the early 1930s they cost £100 each! That was like two years of my total wages! On sporting days the ghillies and the gamies all cycled in, some coming from many miles around; they would meet G.F. and the gentry at eight or eight-thirty in the morning. We had to make sandwiches for the ghillies and get them a bottle of beer from the pantry; the cook, of course, did the lunch boxes for the toffs. The chauffeurs took them to the riverbank, or as far as possible up to the grouse moors, and a local farmer would then take everything up to the top of the hill. One particular farmer was an ex-gamie who knew all the ground in his area like the back of his hand. Well, one day the butler went up the hill with the food and went and laid a cloth on what he thought was the best spot for the gents' lunch, a nice green spot — but the farmer told him it was bog, and that any heavy weight would cause a real problem. But this fool of a butler just carried on and the result was a disaster! G.F. swore at him for not listening to the farmer.

"G.F. was very well thought of in the whole area. He would invite all the local farmers and Grantown businessmen for low ground shooting, and they used to enjoy themselves with rabbits and hares. He was a very generous man, and he gave all of us staff salmon, pheasants, grouse and often a good cut of meat, whichever was in season. My mother always wrote and said thank you, we all wrote, and G.F. really valued these letters from our working-class parents. He was a great benefactor to the local orphanage, and when his wife's fingers got too stiff to play the grand piano, he donated it to the community. He also subsidised lessons for any child who showed outstanding musical ability, in case he or she had the talent to get right to the top. In fact any child who was gifted or showed promise at anything at all was helped as much as possible.

"Mind you, all this goodness didn't always mean that I personally had a good life. I've already said how hard we used to work, in that kitchen from six in the morning, all day until eleven-thirty at night. And I wasn't always treated right, either. For instance, the stove was a huge, heavy, old-fashioned thing with an independent boiler that was used to heat the water. As scullery maid I had to stoke it, and once, when I was barely fifteen years of age, on a Saturday morning the water was stone cold. Well, I knew I'd stoked that boiler well, besides which the kitchen was like an oven. But of course, everyone cursed because there was no hot water, and they all blamed me! This went on all weekend; on Monday a plumber was brought in from Elgin but could find nothing wrong. Then on the Monday night G.F was out at the front door and heard water running: investigating, he found that the hot water tap in a downstairs toilet was fully on. Evidently Mr George Wood, his grandson, had been fishing on Friday night, had used it to wash, and had obviously left the tap on. That was the cause of the entire problem and all my distress.

"Well, G.F. wrote me a nicely written apology — but I have to say, it galled me that nothing was said to the housemaid who had never been near that toilet to clean it. And truth be told, I don't think one note really made up for all the misery I'd suffered.

"There were other things to my mind wrong, too. All the guests who stayed tipped the butler, the footmen, the housemaids and anybody that they came into contact with — but the kitchen staff got nothing. It also upset all of us the way that English and Scottish staff were treated different. We Scottish girls only got two weeks' holiday a year and had to pay all our fares backwards and forwards. English girls, on the other hand, got three weeks' holiday and had their fares paid. There were some bitter arguments about that, I can tell you.

"G.F.'s grandson, Mr George Wood — who was responsible for the hot water incident — died when he was fifty-six years old, from throat cancer; he had several operations, but nothing helped. He was a nice-looking gent he was, and good to us. In 1932, I remember, he came to stay with G.F. and Mrs McCorquodale. One night there was a dance, and he took charge of all the dancing and even came through to the servants' hall to make sure that everyone had partners. I was coming from the kitchen with more lemonade, and he took me up to an eightsome reel and later to an old-fashioned waltz. These were the only two dances that he had that night, and the housemaids were furious to think that he would lower his dignity and dance with a kitchen maidie!

"A year ago I went back to the house. It's called Tulchan now, after the original lodge which was tiny with small rooms and was eventually flattened. It is currently owned by people in plastic, and they're really making it pay; it's a magnificent place. All I could recognise from the 1930s were the front and back doors! Everything now has all mod cons, and the furniture, too, is truly magnificent. Mind you, bed and breakfast costs hundreds of pounds a night! The butler's quarters today are where we slept as maids. The factor gave me the same present as that presented to Nick Faldo, the golfing personality: it was like a family Bible, the exterior all the same shape in lovely shades of green and with gold leaf, but inside was a flagon of mature whisky and two goblets. It seems that I'm the only old servant of the McCorquodales that they have met.

"When I was there, looking at the garden brought back another memory. One year an Irish tinkle [tinker] came and did an Irish jig out on the lawn, all dressed up in traditional clothes. Well, G.F. enjoyed it so much that he gave the tinker £25 each year just to come and dance. All of us staff were invited to watch, and by Jove, yon fellow could really do an Irish jig! I don't think we'll ever see his like again — or, for that matter, the likes of G.F."

The sun was setting majestically across the grounds of the hotel, and the sea in the distance sparkled in the evening light. I asked Janet why she had not stayed with the McCorquodales.

"I don't really know that. Probably I just felt it was time to move on — and remember, I couldn't get any more money there. So I applied for, and got a job — again as a kitchen maid — with Lady Rochdale at Lingholm House, a huge place in Keswick, in Cumberland; Lord Rochdale was a clothing manufacturer. He employed six hundred in his mills; at one time Gracie Fields was on his payroll! He was also the Lord Lieutenant of Liverpool, and actually opened the Mersey Tunnel himself. However, he had been severely injured in the 1914-18 war and could only walk a few inches aided by two sticks. He employed a Mr Ward to be his constant companion and aide, and a chauffeur called Simpkins; he had a Rolls-Royce with a specially made back seat, which you could turn into a bed. Simpkins was a dreadful man; he used to come in at night blind drunk, and he'd cause all sorts of trouble in the kitchen with his drunken ways.

"One night Lord Rochdale went to bed early, but saw a light in the garage. Although it was about a quarter of a mile to walk, he made it on his sticks and caught Simpkins siphoning petrol out of the Rolls. He gave him the sack on the spot, with half an hour to gather his belongings and no pay. Simpkins had let his master down after twenty-five years of service; never again would he get a chauffeur's job.

"My last job in England was as an undercook, with the Duke and Duchess of Gloucester at the Royal Pavilion in Aldershot. My very last job in service, just before the outbreak of World War II, was at Invergloy House, owned by a millionairess, a Miss Jamie Allan. There wasn't quite such a big staff here, but Miss Allan's people had once owned the Cunard Line. Miss Allan was to have sailed on the maiden voyage of the *Titanic*, but she had a friend who was very ill; Miss Allan went to nurse her, and therefore possibly saved her own life by doing so.

"I remember especially the furniture in this house: it was beautiful, very light, and a lot of it inlaid with walnut; the dining-room table was huge, a great slab of oak dating from the time of Cromwell. The curtains in that room were over two hundred years old, a lovely chenille velvet, rich red in colour. Miss Allan had a brush covered in velvet, and she used this herself to keep the curtains clean; none of us girls was allowed to touch them. Her drawing room was sixty feet long, and she had had a cabinetmaker fit a beautiful cupboard that measured exactly the length of the room, and over the years she had filled it with miniatures from all over the world; once she said to me that if she lost all her money, this cabinet with all the wee shepherdesses and dolls would keep her going for the rest of her life. She dusted all these miniatures herself, saying that if any were broken then she'd only have herself to blame. We breathed a sigh of relief over that, I can tell you!

"Miss Allan lived until she was a hundred years old, and in the end lived in two chauffeurs' houses that were made into one. She paid all her staff insurance — she would pay anything to avoid income tax, which she considered to be the bane of her life. And if any child on the estate needed specialist treatment, then Miss Allan would pay for it. During the last war one of the gardener's sons was a despatch rider when France was falling; he was blown through a plate-glass window, and the French surgeons were preparing to take his leg off. But when Miss Allan was told, she sent an ambulance to France with surgeons, doctors and two nurses, and they saved Freddie's leg!

"I don't think we'll ever see her like again. Nor, come to that, any of my previous employers. Today, it's a different way of life in every sense. For better or for worse I just don't know."

Janet's story is peopled by the rich, the famous and the eccentric, aristocrats whose social rank gave them almost total domination over the lives of the domestic staff they employed. Long periods of indifference could be punctuated by acts of amazing charity and kindness — but as Janet ruefully observed, in not one of the kitchens she worked in was there any sort of first-aid kit: so fingers were cut and blood was spilt, and servants quickly developed a healthy respect for the kitchen knife. A small point, perhaps, but that's how it was in those days: staff were expendable, and in the Hungry Thirties if you didn't like a job or it was too much for you, then you could be sure there was somebody else on the doorstep ready to take it over.

Back at her residential home, one of the attendants was looking out anxiously for Janet as the light waned and the winter afternoon gave way to dusk. Not unexpectedly, Janet is a favourite amongst the residents, and some were already gathering round to hear about her day; so we said goodbye and I was awarded a kiss on each cheek. And assuredly I shall always value the day we spent together, sharing such wonderful memories.

A Changing Structure

The social structure of Great Britain has changed enormously since the heyday of the great estates; the very rigid hierarchy observed amongst the servants themselves, and the unbending relationship between master and servant has given way to a freer informality between employer and employee.

In mapping this social change it is revealing to consider the lifestyle of two people employed in service in the first half of the twentieth century, in somewhat less prestigious houses: Margaret, a personal maid, and May Moore, who worked her whole life in service. The final story of Mr Robertson, David and Doreen goes to show that the hiring of personal staff today is not always the blessing it might seem to be . . .

Margaret, Personal Maid

My mother had her own personal maid, a young girl called Margaret, when she was a teenager. My grandfather was not titled, nor was he fabulously well off, but he was still able to afford a modest household staff.

Margaret and my mother were almost of the same age — Margaret just two years my mother's senior — and they were apparently inseparable. After leaving school, Margaret had jumped at the chance of moving to a large house in the fashionable suburbs.

Her duties were comparatively light: she lit my mother's bedroom fire during the cold months of the year; she would put out clothes for the day, and prepare special gowns for evening occasions. She would also help wash my mother's hair, which at that time reached right down past her waist.

Other duties might include cleaning jewellery, taking the family dog for a walk, doing any shopping of a personal nature for my mother, and most importantly, simply being there. In short, Margaret became my mother's best and most trusted friend. Money had little or nothing to do with this: the two girls simply had a close, relaxed and affectionate relationship.

Margaret worked for my mother right up until the outbreak of World War II; then my mother finally left home to get married, and to follow her new husband away to his posting in Scotland. Margaret went into the local factory, making goods vital to the war effort. Until this separation, Margaret was always there as help and support to my mother. For instance, my mother had been on the point of engagement some years before her eventual first marriage, but her boyfriend had been killed, tragically, in a car crash. She always remembered Margaret's support over the following days: when my mother was awake — which was nearly always — so was Margaret; if she didn't eat, nor did Margaret — only after forty-eight hours did they take any food. It was Margaret who helped my mother through the funeral, and it was she who taught my mother eventually to face life again.

It was much the same early in the war. My mother had an adored brother, Martin, who went down with his torpedoed ship. As soon as the news reached home, Margaret was on that train to Invergordon in the east of Scotland to provide comfort once more.

Not that it was always like that: Margaret thoroughly enjoyed the parties, the dinners, the Christmases — in short, being a treasured part of a household that had a life far more glamorous than any she had experienced before. My mother and Margaret kept in touch until the mid-fifties, by which time she had a happy and contented life with three children.

May Moore

Mary Burkett has compiled the life history of May Moore, and in so doing has given us a vivid insight into the social history of this century. The short life of this woman who devoted herself to service describes perfectly the sort of career that is now all but forgotten.

May was born in 1907 on the fringes of the Lake District. By the age of eight, she was already employed at Isel Hall after the school day was done. At Isel she cleaned brasses, particularly stubborn stoves and the fringes of the dining-room carpet where dirt could be seen. If this were not enough, her weekends were employed at the local almshouse where she cleaned out the grates, and it was not an easy task removing the more stubborn ashes.

The only time that May ever rebelled in her young life she was severely punished for it: she was twelve years of age, and one day at school she omitted to curtsey to the head master, for which she was given two strokes of the cane. She fainted and was carried from the building by two of the boys who placed her close to a bridge near a ditch; from this she fell off into the stream, hitting her head and becoming drenched. She was found by a passer-by who took her to Cockermouth cottage hospital where she was treated for three days. Times have certainly changed since 1919!

At thirteen, May left school and went to Isel full time as an under parlour maid. Her duties included waiting at table and learning how to serve food correctly, and tidying the downstairs rooms. She also had to clean four fireplaces before breakfast, often having to get up at 5.30 in the morning to do this. Also before breakfast she had to iron the newspapers — yes, iron the newspapers! After breakfast she cleaned the bedrooms upstairs, then polished up the kitchen stoves. This work was desperately hard — she had to clean all the old panels with vinegar until they gleamed. For this — generally at least twelve hours' work a day — she was paid the princely sum of just under £2 per month. I wonder if it was any consolation that she had ten days holiday per year!

Not that everything was drudgery: at the age of fifteen she learned to drive Sir Wilfred Lawson's Daimler, though because she was still so small she had to be propped up with two cushions in order to reach the wheel! In the early days, she needed someone to change gears for her so that she could concentrate on the steering! Three times a week she drove into Carlisle, for fish for breakfast and for medicine at the chemist. Fortunately in those days there was next to no traffic whatsoever on the roads. May's own summary of those days is succinct: "I had to do my work properly and polish the silver well. That was the way we were taught, and we never had to answer back."

In her thirties, May went to work in Basingstoke in Hampshire and was a lady's maid there to Lady Gibb. This was really a taste of the high life and three times a week she and the family went into London in a Rolls-Royce, May looking after the jewel box which perched on her knee. Needless to say, the attractions of London were beyond May's pocket, especially as all her surplus money was sent back home to her mother and her sister; May contented herself with walking into St James's Park to see the wildlife.

Her mother's illness obliged her to return to Coniston in the Lake District where she could be close by; here, once again, she moved into service as a lady's maid. It was during this period of her life that she came to know Beatrix Potter well: one day there was a knock at the door, and a plumpish lady in a shabby tweed suit came in, asking May whether she cut hair. This was a great lady! The two women struck up a lively relationship, and May would carry out all sorts of small tasks for the world-famous author; darning, fixing a hem, all sorts of small tasks like this were rewarded by a bar of chocolate, an apple pie, and once an original drawing of Peter Rabbit, the value of which was never appreciated.

Money was scarce, even at this later period of May's life. On one occasion Beatrix Potter asked May for aspirin, so she went into the local town to buy a packet. She was given an apple pie in exchange, Beatrix Potter obviously failing to appreciate that even a few aspirin caused a serious dent in such a frugal budget.

May's life did become easier as her family grew around her, and took their turn in caring for her. She even travelled to New Zealand in her older age! Mary Burkett writes: "Rarely will you come across someone whose face lights up with such delight when looking back on life devoted to serving others." This is how May and many others like her lived their lives.

Times were changing, however, and a memory of Violet Ward reinforces this. As a child, Violet lived in the imposing observatory tower at Gunton Hall in Norfolk, home to the Suffield family, and she recalls the time one of the Ward cousins came to stay. Lady Suffield often approached the hall through the gates within the observatory tower, and Violet's family were expected to curtsey when she appeared. But the cousin would have nothing to do with this: "I will curtsey to no one!" she said. "My mother has told me that I need never curtsey to any one in my life now." Indeed the Great War had been and gone, and social values were changed forever.

Master and Servant in Modern Times

As we move towards the end of the twentieth century it is evident that the relationship between master and servant takes on many different forms. Quite recently I was invited to attend a fishing party in the Highlands where one of the guests was a very rich banker; he had been driven up from London by his chauffeur, whom we will call Robertson (I think for everybody's sake it is important to keep the real identity secret!)

The two men appeared a little before dinner squabbling rather like an irritable married couple. The banker was peevish, accusing Robertson of getting lost on purpose simply to be annoying: "You wanted to make me late just so I would miss an afternoon's fishing!"

Robertson was equally aggressive: "If you say one more thing to me then I'm off, and you can drive your bloody car back to London yourself!" And he stormed out of the house and went to the isolated public house where he drank till midnight, came home singing and woke up the entire household. A furious argument between him and the banker ensued, the banker threatening dismissal and Robertson resignation.

For the rest of the week the two never spoke at all, and if any messages had to be relayed it was through others. For example, I had to ask Robertson if he would drive into Inverness to buy more flies and fishing line. This he did, grudgingly, but he was away the whole day so once again the banker had to curtail his fishing. When eventually their stay was over and they drove off you could hear them still arguing. However, our host observed that they had been together for well over twenty-five years, and he'd never known them different.

Our host had brought with him his own chauffeur, David; the latter's wife Doreen acted as housekeeper.

Their show of deference and obedience was veneer thin: when David said "Sir", it was with a sneer that made your flesh creep; when Doreen did anything it was with a heaving sigh that instantly made you apologise for troubling her.

They would spend the whole day in the kitchen, pattering away, criticising their employer and all the guests, drinking sherry by the bottle and producing a barely edible dinner in a very tipsy fashion. The guests were expected to help clear the table and take the dishes into the kitchen where David and Doreen would be washing up in the most laboured fashion. "Nearly the end of another hard day," Doreen would say to him. "Yes, love, but we're up again before dawn as usual," he would reply. Meanwhile it was quite obvious to all that the best bottle of port was sitting on the sink top, rapidly disappearing down their fatigued gullets!

INDEX

ISIS publish a wide range of books in large print, from fiction to biography. A full list of titles is available free of charge from the address below. Alternatively, contact your local library for details of their collection of ISIS large print books.

Details of ISIS complete and unabridged audio books are also available.

Any suggestions for books you would like to see in large print or audio are always welcome.

ISIS

7 Centremead
Osney Mead
Oxford OX2 0ES
(01865) 250333